best ever

quick & easy

p

This is a Parragon Book
This edition published in 2004

Parragon
Queen Street House
4 Queen Street
Bath BA1 1HE
United Kingdom

Created and produced by
The Bridgewater Book Company Ltd,
Lewes, East Sussex

Photographer Ian Parsons
Home economists Sara Hesketh and Richard Green

ISBN: 1-40542-043-X

Printed in China

NOTE

This book uses metric and imperial measurements. Follow the same units
of measurement throughout; do not mix metric and imperial. All spoon
measurements are level: teaspoons are assumed to be 5 ml and tablespoons
are assumed to be 15 ml. Unless otherwise stated, milk is assumed to be full fat,
eggs and individual vegetables such as potatoes are medium, and pepper is
freshly ground black pepper.

The times given for each recipe are an approximate guide only because
the preparation times may differ according to the techniques used by
different people and the cooking times may vary as a result of the type of
oven used. Ovens should be preheated to the specified temperature. If using
a fan-assisted oven, check the manufacturer's instructions for adjusting the time
and temperature. The preparation times include chilling and marinating times,
where appropriate.

The nutritional information provided for each recipe is per serving or
per portion. Optional ingredients, variations or serving suggestions have
not been included in the calculations.

Recipes using raw or very lightly cooked eggs should be avoided
by infants, the elderly, pregnant women, convalescents and anyone
suffering from an illness.

contents

introduction
4

soups & starters
14

salads & snacks
78

meat & poultry
120

fish & shellfish
170

desserts
210

index
254

introduction

Many people have hectic, busy lives these days with little time or desire to cook complicated meals every day. An increasing reliance on takeaway foods, however convenient, can become expensive and unhealthy. This book demonstrates methods, tips and tricks for cooking fast, simple, tasty and nutritious meals, mostly at little expense. Even if you do not generally enjoy cooking, you will find very easy recipes that even the worst cook will be pleased with at the end. Many of the recipes featured are low fat and all are healthy and nutritious – essential for busy lifestyles that require lots of energy and vitality. When meals are cooked in just a few minutes, this leaves time to sit comfortably, relax and enjoy your food, reducing the risk of indigestion – a common problem for those who frequently eat 'on the run'. Step-by-step instructions and photographs of the key stages of preparation make the recipes easy to follow, ensuring that this book is a must for every busy person's kitchen.

Many of the recipes featured take less than 30 minutes from kitchen to table and some take even less time, allowing you to enjoy your creation, whether on your own or with a large group of friends and family. Each recipe includes an at-a-glance reference to the time it takes to prepare, although this will vary depending on your expertise, and the time it takes to cook. Most dishes can be served immediately, but a few benefit from being made in advance and chilled; this is flagged in the recipe.

Most home-made versions of salads, dressings and sauces are far less expensive than the shop-bought alternatives and are undoubtedly healthier, as you know exactly what ingredients have been added. Preparing food at home can give you a great sense of satisfaction, is much healthier for you and your family and need not be time-consuming and messy. This book shows you an alternative way to ensure that preparing and cooking food is an enjoyable daily activity for you and your family, not a chore to dread or an inconvenience that you have to fit in around everything else.

fabulous fast food

There is a recipe here to suit every course, occasion and family, whether you are single and need a speedy dinner before going out for the evening or have a very large family with disparate activities and hobbies and don't have time for a traditional Sunday roast. Asian dishes are traditionally quick to make and increasingly popular, so many favourites are featured here, such as Sesame Prawn Toasts (see page 54) and Thai Golden Pouches (see page 61), which may be served as snacks or as impressive starters for guests. A recipe that can be adapted in countless ways, Singapore Noodles (see page 107), makes an ideal lunch or light evening meal for those on the run. Stir-fries are renowned for the speed in which they can be prepared and cooked, and Pork Stir-fry (see page 132) is no exception. Chinese and other Asian dishes are also wonderful for entertaining, as you can easily prepare a smaller amount of several dishes and everybody is sure to find something to suit their particular tastes. Cooked using very little oil, they are particularly healthy for those watching their waistlines and cholesterol levels and are popular with people of all ages – from the

very young and
picky to the elderly. The
range is vast: for example, Thai
Fragrant Mussels (see page 209) is simplicity itself and
well worth the cost for a special occasion, whereas
Chinese Chicken (see page 158) is equally easy, yet
economical and so appropriate for very large families.

Many traditional Western dishes are also featured,
such as Old English Cheese Soup (see page 26) and
Mushroom Soup (see page 30) for a light lunch or starter,
and Chicken Cordon Bleu (see page 156) and Finnan
Haddie (see page 177) for a satisfying main course.
Recipes for those who have little time for shopping and
find that they never have the right ingredients include
Storecupboard Tuna (see page 111) and Toad in the Hole
with Onion Gravy (see page 144). Some familiar dishes
from around the world are the popular dips, Hummus
(see page 68) and Guacamole (see page 69) from the
Middle East and Mexico respectively, and the Italian
Spaghetti alla Carbonara (see page 100), Prosciutto & Figs

(see page 74) and Mozzarella & Tomatoes
(see page 75). These are ideal for
entertaining at lunchtime, as is the
French Salade Niçoise (see page 81),
which can be prepared with canned
or fresh tuna and is delicious served
al fresco in the summer.

Many of the dishes
recommended for entertaining
look impressive, but are actually
astonishingly easy to serve, simply
by piling the various ingredients
around and on top of each other in
a decorative way. There are also more
unusual and unfamiliar dishes that, at
first glance, seem to require long and
tedious preparation or special
equipment, but which turn out to be far
easier and quicker than you would think.
Experiment with new flavours or rediscover
classics – try Russian Salad (see page 88) or Chef's
Salad (see page 86) in the summer or for a light meal,
and Tournedos Rossini (see page 125), Chicken Teriyaki
(see page 157) or Tarragon Chicken (see page 161) for
a more filling dish. If you are a fan of fish and seafood,
whether eating alone or throwing a dinner party, try Sole
Meunière (see page 183), Veracruz Red Snapper (see page
186) or the Louisiana speciality Blackened Fish (see page
174). For something a little more exotic, try Thai Prawn
Curry (see page 202) or Balti Prawns (see page 203).

Special desserts can also be quick and easy – you do
not have to limit yourself to ice cream or fresh fruit. There
are many desserts, both hot and cold, that are simple,
healthy and interesting. Refreshing and cooling Indian
Mango Dessert (see page 222) is the ideal choice after
a spicy curry or stir-fry and it is great as a summer snack
as well. Many of these desserts, such as Zabaglione (see
page 234) and Strawberry Baked Alaska (see page 241),
look as if they have taken a lot of time and effort to

prepare, yet are so simple that they almost seem like cheating. If you are fond of fruit and also have a sweet tooth, then you may want to try the Fruit Parcels (see page 238), Lemon Posset (see page 242), Speedy Apricot Cheesecake (see page 246) or Fried Bananas in Maple Syrup (see page 248). These are just a few of the delicious desserts featured and you are sure to find one to complement the rest of the meal.

time-saving tips

There are many different ways to save time in the kitchen and you can use some or all of the methods together for really fast food. Quick and easy meals are very often highly nutritious, as the cooking methods preserve many of the important nutrients, particularly in vegetables.

Fast food techniques are nothing new – people have always been busy. In countries such as China, where historically fuel was scarce, this was an extra incentive to develop a way of cooking quickly, which resulted in the invention of the wok and stir-frying. Grilling, griddling, pan-frying and stir-frying are the best techniques for cooking food quickly while preserving texture, colour and flavour. Some ingredients, such as chops and steaks, are best suited to grilling or griddling and others, such as chicken breast portions, can be cooked using whichever method suits you. Other options include poaching and baking in a parcel – moderately fast techniques that are especially suitable for cooking chicken, fish and fruit. Use the recipes in this book as a guide to the best ways of cooking ingredients, as well as the best ways of presenting and serving them.

If you are used to a diet of slow-cooked casseroles or meat and two veg and you find that time is just not on your side, then you may have to re-educate yourself to produce fast and easy meals – for midweek family suppers anyway. Thinly sliced, diced, chopped or grated ingredients cook significantly faster than chunky or whole

ones and also look attractive. Cooking vegetables this way makes them even healthier and preserves their texture.

Running a household, holding down a job and feeding a family can be difficult to balance, so apply a little lateral thinking: you may find that one-pot meals are an ideal solution. They create less washing-up, make less mess in the kitchen in general and often involve less chopping and peeling than many other dishes. If you are not fortunate enough to have a dishwasher, clearing up at the end of a meal can often mean standing at the sink for long periods of time when you are full, tired and need to get on with something else.

Often overlooked, one of the easiest ways to save time when cooking is not to – in other words, to serve raw ingredients. As a main course or side dish, salads are the perfect choice – quick, easy, nutritious and attractive. However, making the most of uncooked ingredients is not just limited to salads. You can serve raw vegetables, such as grated carrots, or canned mixed beans with cooked chicken or pasta dishes. Fresh bread and rolls are traditional accompaniments to meals throughout Europe, a pleasant habit worth adopting. Cheese requires little or no preparation and is ideal for adding flavour, colour, texture and substance to any meal. You can buy packets of ready-grated cheese at most supermarkets, although these are not so nice as freshly grated cheese. Parmesan and pecorino are perfect for adding a strong flavour to dishes and should be bought fresh in small quantities and grated as required.

Remember that you don't have to perform like a celebrity chef on television when you are in your own kitchen. Most of us cannot safely wield a chopping knife at that kind of speed and it isn't always necessary. Ingredients such as ham, bacon, chives, dill, sun-dried tomatoes and anchovies can be snipped straight into the saucepan using a pair of kitchen scissors, saving time and cutting down on washing-up.

Storecupboard ingredients in jars and cans are invaluable for quick meals and you can make a satisfactory lunch or dinner using these alone. Consider canned ingredients, such as chopped tomatoes, baby sweetcorn and sliced mushrooms, as rapid alternatives to fresh ingredients. Canned pulses, such as mixed beans, kidney beans, lentils and chickpeas, save an enormous amount of preparation time and are inexpensive. Olives, capers and anchovies are great tossed into a salad to make it more interesting or can be roughly chopped and added to many other dishes. Add capers sparingly, as they have a strong, pickled taste. Olives can be used as a garnish or as part of the dish; try both black olives and stuffed green olives, as they have very different flavours. Both go well with fish, including canned tuna and salmon. Canned fish can be the basis for a lunch or light dinner and needs only to be drained and flaked. Tuna, salmon, anchovy fillets, crabmeat and sardines are valuable storecupboard stand-bys. You can base an entire meal around them or just add them to a vegetable dish for extra flavour, colour and protein. Sardines are rather oily, but the valuable omega-3 essential fatty acids are extremely good for you and the fish are tasty straight from the can, combined with a potato dish or salad. Most nuts will keep relatively well in a sealed container and can be used as a quick and easy garnish, but buy them in small quantities, as they will turn rancid if kept too long. Peanuts can also be used for a satay sauce or snack food, and pine kernels, walnuts and cashew nuts can all be added to food while cooking or sprinkled over before serving.

Ready-prepared vegetables are now widely available and are a great timesaver when you are entertaining, especially for recipes requiring carrots cut into thin batons, cauliflower broken into small florets and similar fiddly foods. Many of these vegetables, which include carrots, baby sweetcorn, mangetout, cauliflower and salads, can be eaten raw and will look attractive simply removed from their packaging and arranged on a serving plate. They are ideal for serving with dips at parties.

Buying ready washed and trimmed vegetables is also a great timesaver and you may find these ingredients for almost the same price as unprepared varieties. The main disadvantage is that once vegetables have been cut, they begin to lose their nutrients.

Many ready-made sauces can be used as instant flavouring for a variety of dishes and even those usually offered as condiments at the table can make interesting additions. Try mustard added to beef or chicken recipes and Worcestershire sauce added to soups and strongly flavoured dishes. Many Asian sauces can be used for recipes other than those of Asian origin and there is a wide range available, including soy, hoisin, plum, black bean and oyster sauce as well as Thai fish (also known as nam pla). Many of these Asian sauces are very strong and you need only a few drops. Light soy sauce has a saltier, weaker flavour and paler colour than dark soy sauce – use it in a dish that requires no extra colouring. Dark soy sauce has a sweeter flavour and much darker colour and adds an exotic touch to vegetable, rice and noodle dishes as well as meat. No extra salt need be added to dishes with soy sauce in them. Tabasco sauce is made in Louisiana, the home of many spicy dishes. It can be added to soups, sauces and braises to add moderate or fiery heat and is an easy alternative to chopping fresh chillies.

Dried mushrooms add an intense flavour to other ingredients, making the cost worthwhile. Using concentrated flavourings eliminates the need to reduce sauces – tomato purée, sun-dried tomatoes, bottled lemon juice and stock cubes or bouillon powder add the flavour required without increasing the preparation or cooking time. For the best flavour, look for stock cubes that do not have too much added salt. Tomato purée is concentrated and you will need to add only a little to your cooking for a strong flavour and colour. Sun-dried tomato paste is also readily available in most large supermarkets and makes wonderfully flavoursome sauces.

It has a darker colour than standard tomato purée and a stronger, more distinctive flavour, so use sparingly. If you use tomato paste (sun-dried or normal) regularly, buy a jar, but as it can go mouldy quickly, buying a small tube may be more economical. Store in the refrigerator.

Passata is an Italian alternative to canned tomatoes. It is made from sieved tomatoes and is smoother than canned tomatoes. It makes a great base for sauces and soups and can be added to casseroles and stews with delicious results.

Pasta is an ideal foundation for many quick dishes, as it takes very little time to cook and requires no preparation. Fresh pasta can cook in as little as 2–3 minutes and most people find it tastier than dried varieties. However, dried pasta is a useful storecupboard stand-by and is ready to serve within about 10 minutes. There are plenty of dried pasta varieties to choose from, such as tagliatelle, fusilli and farfalle, as well as ready-made sauces. These are useful if your time is limited and you want a very quick dish which is tasty and nutritious. Many dishes traditionally served with potatoes, which take longer to cook, can be adapted to be served with pasta instead.

An Asian alternative to pasta, noodles are convenient, cook quickly and are healthy. They store well and will keep for a long time. Use noodles in soups and stir-fries and flavour with sesame oil and soy sauce. The easiest to buy and cook are egg noodles, which are inexpensive and come dried, usually in rectangular cakes. Rice noodles are also easy to cook and are available from many Asian supermarkets. As the name suggests, they are made from rice flour. Most noodles are of medium thickness, although you may find thicker ones in an Asian supermarket. Long, thin noodles are best used in soups and also in light sauces.

A fast and easy way to cook potatoes is in the microwave, this method being particularly suited to baked potatoes. In fact, most things, from meat to sauces, can be cooked in the microwave, although some foods are more suitable than others. Many foods will cook in around a quarter of the time they would take using conventional methods, and a microwave is very useful for thawing frozen complete dishes or individual ingredients. Although a microwave may save you time with many dishes, you may find you still have to stop and stir certain ingredients and foods, such as gravy and custard. Unlike a conventional oven, the more you put in the microwave, the longer it will take to cook, making it impractical for speedy meals. The microwave is a short-cut for softening butter, melting chocolate and bringing citrus fruits to room temperature before squeezing.

forward planning

There is an old army saying that time spent in reconnaissance is never wasted and this is as true in the kitchen as it is on the front line. Being well organized and properly prepared in the kitchen is all the more important if you are short of time. Planning menus in advance avoids those occasions when you wander around the kitchen, poking about in the refrigerator and rummaging in cupboards, wondering what to cook. Sit down at the weekend or before you go shopping with a pen and paper and plan the meals you are going to cook for the whole week. Don't begrudge the few minutes this will take you, as it will help you to feel more in control and more confident that you will succeed in getting meals ready in time and with the minimum of effort.

Shop selectively and plan properly. If you are planning a dish with a sauce, such as pesto, can you buy a palatable version of the sauce ready-made instead of making one yourself? Alternatively, if you use a particular sauce frequently, consider making a large batch in advance and storing it in convenient portions in the freezer. Jars of minced garlic are a time-saving alternative to fresh garlic and are usually very tasty. You can also buy root ginger, coriander and some other herbs in jars; as long as you like the flavour, they save a lot of time and effort. However, bear in mind that it is sometimes not worth sacrificing flavour or texture for time. Are you really sure that powdered mashed potato is as nice as the real thing? Remember, too, to buy ingredients that you can use in more than one recipe, even in the same meal – soured cream can go with a starter and into a main course or crème fraîche can thicken a sauce for a main course and then be served with fruit for dessert. This saves a surprising amount of time that is often wasted finding ingredients, opening pots, adding and mixing, and also eliminates wastage.

Having a well-organized storecupboard and refrigerator is essential for making sure that you know where all the required ingredients are and to avoid having to stop to clear up spills caused by over-reaching for inaccessible items. It also helps avoid waste and disappointment, as you are less likely to overlook use-by dates on cans and packets or to leave something unidentified mouldering into a new and furry life form in the salad drawer of the refrigerator.

Make sure that you have an adequate range of basic equipment, such as sharp knives, sieves, colanders, wooden spoons and good-quality saucepans, as these will aid you in the speedy preparation of ingredients. Sharp knives are safer than blunt ones, too. Chopping boards are an essential item and will last a very long time. Invest in two, one for raw meat and seafood and the other for vegetables and cooked ingredients, as this will save your having to stop to clean a single board. Whether you prefer wood or plastic, select a good, solid board that will not slip easily.

Good-quality, heavy-based saucepans are valuable investments, as they will ensure that the heat is evenly distributed through the saucepan, cooking your food faster and more evenly.

A wok is ideal for many quick dishes, not only those of Asian origin. The design ensures that the food is cooked evenly and it can be placed over a very high heat, but it is important to buy a good-quality cast-iron wok, not a non-stick one, as the latter are not so reliable at very high temperatures. If you cook on an electric hob with a flat surface, select a wok with a flat base. A thick, solid base is very important to allow even distribution of heat. If the instructions tell you to season a wok before use, do so, as this improves the quality of cooking and the wok will last longer.

A ridged griddle pan makes an attractive pattern on steaks and chops and can be used for many things, from kebabs to fish steaks. Buy cast-iron to ensure quality and make sure that you look after your kitchen equipment so that it lasts.

A solid, heavy-based, flameproof casserole can be costly, but is worth the money, as meals will be evenly cooked, moist and flavoursome. You can use it on top of the stove to cook onions and sear meat at the beginning of a recipe and then to cook the rest of the dish, whether on the hob or in the oven, saving time and effort in both preparation and clearing up afterwards.

A steamer is a healthy way of cooking food and will not make vegetables, such as broccoli and cabbage, go soggy. It leaves them with a lovely texture and colour and is useful for cooking more than one item at a time. You can set a steamer over a saucepan of water in which you have potatoes cooking and cook your broccoli and carrots in it, thereby cooking three things at once. Besides saving you time and energy, this is a more economical way of using fuel, too. As with any method of cooking, you can overcook in a steamer, but it is much harder to do so than by boiling for too long.

Measuring jugs and spoons with clear, easy-to-read numbers are important. Although many dishes will not suffer from guesswork, some require exact measurements. Make sure you have metric and imperial measurements, but remember that they are not interchangeable.

There are many labour-saving kitchen tools on the market, most of which are inexpensive and readily available, but some tools are more useful than others. An electric can opener, for example, will save you a couple of seconds, while a food processor or electric whisk will save valuable minutes.

A solidly constructed, swivel-blade vegetable peeler is not only the easiest alternative to buying ready-peeled vegetables, but can be used for Parmesan and pecorino cheese shavings for an easy, attractive garnish.

Using a citrus zester is far easier than trying to grate lemon, lime or orange rind and then scrape it from the inside of the grater.

Whatever equipment you are buying for the kitchen, from soup ladle to potato masher, choose good-quality brands with a reputable name, and care for and clean it properly to ensure that it will last you well. In addition, make sure that you have adequate storage space and that you have thought out where everything goes. Keep sharp knives, wooden spoons and chopping boards near the work surface or in drawers underneath it and store saucepans and woks near the stove. Save yourself lots of time and energy by planning your kitchen and keeping it clean and tidy: you do not want to be walking a marathon backwards and forwards across the kitchen in the middle of preparing dinner.

time-saving check list

- If you will need to use the oven or grill, switch it on to preheat the moment you walk into the kitchen. Skimping on preheating doesn't save time and can increase the risk of food poisoning through inadequate cooking.

- Read the recipe before you begin. You can save time by preparing some ingredients while others are cooking. Onions, for example, take at least 5 minutes to soften in a frying pan of oil, so use this time to slice the meat, chop the carrots or open a can of tomatoes.

- Fresh salad leaves and delicate herbs, such as basil, bruise easily if sliced or chopped with a knife – it is both better and quicker to tear or shred them with your fingers.

- Using the appropriate size of saucepan for the ingredients makes cooking easier and quicker. There is no point heating up more liquid than you require or trying to stir an over-filled saucepan and constantly splashing the hob and possibly yourself.

- When cutting soft, creamy cheese, rinse the knife blade in cold water first to prevent sticking. This saves time and also prevents an uneven appearance.

- Mix Vinaigrette (see page 13) and other salad dressings in a screw-top jar by shaking them vigorously together. You can store any leftover dressing in the jar in the refrigerator for 2–3 days.

- Strip blackcurrants and redcurrants from their stems by running the tines of a fork along the stem. Strip small leaves from herb sprigs by running the stem between your thumb and forefinger.

- Foods cook more rapidly in metal or china containers than in earthenware or glass.

- If you prefer to make basic stocks, dressings and vinaigrettes yourself, then the recipes opposite can all be made in advance. The stocks can be stored in the freezer for 3–6 months and the vinaigrettes and dressings can be kept in screw-top jars in the refrigerator for 2–3 days. Shake or stir well before using.

basic recipes

vegetable stock

makes: about 2 litres/3½ pints
preparation time: 10 minutes
cooking time: 35 minutes

2 tbsp sunflower or corn oil
115 g/4 oz onions, finely chopped
115 g/4 oz leeks, finely chopped
115 g/4 oz carrots, finely chopped
4 celery sticks, finely chopped
85 g/3 oz fennel, finely chopped
85 g/3 oz tomatoes, finely chopped
2.25 litres/4 pints water
1 bouquet garni

1 Heat the oil in a saucepan. Add the onions and leeks and cook over a low heat for 5 minutes, or until softened. Add the remaining vegetables, cover and cook for 10 minutes. Add the water and bouquet garni, bring to the boil and simmer for 20 minutes.

2 Sieve, cool and store in the refrigerator. Use immediately or freeze in portions for up to 3 months.

chicken stock

makes: about 2.5 litres/4½ pints
preparation time: 15 minutes, plus 30 minutes chilling
cooking time: 3½ hours

1.3 kg/3 lb chicken wings and necks
2 onions, cut into wedges
4 litres/7 pints water
2 carrots, roughly chopped
2 celery sticks, roughly chopped
10 fresh parsley sprigs
4 fresh thyme sprigs
2 bay leaves
10 black peppercorns

1 Place the chicken wings and necks and the onions in a large, heavy-based saucepan and cook over a low heat, stirring frequently, until lightly browned.

2 Add the water and stir to scrape off any sediment on the base of the saucepan. Bring to the boil, skimming off

any foam that rises to the surface. Add the remaining ingredients, partially cover and simmer gently for 3 hours.

3 Sieve, cool and place in the refrigerator. When cold, discard the layer of fat on the surface. Use immediately or freeze in portions for up to 6 months.

beef stock

makes: about 1.7 litres/3 pints
preparation time: 15 minutes, plus 30 minutes chilling
cooking time: 4½ hours

1 kg/2 lb 4 oz beef marrow bones, sawn into 7.5-cm/3-inch pieces
650 g/1 lb 7 oz stewing beef in 1 piece
2.8 litres/5 pints water
4 cloves
2 onions, halved
2 celery sticks, roughly chopped
8 peppercorns
1 bouquet garni

1 Place the bones in the base of a large saucepan and place the stewing beef on top. Add the water and bring to the boil over a low heat, skimming off any foam that rises to the surface.

2 Press a clove into each onion half and add to the pan with the celery, peppercorns and bouquet garni. Partially cover and simmer very gently for 3 hours. Remove the meat and simmer for 1 hour.

3 Sieve, cool and place in the refrigerator. When cold, discard the layer of fat on the surface. Use immediately or freeze in portions for up to 6 months.

vinaigrette

makes: about 225 ml/8 fl oz
preparation time: 5 minutes, plus 1 hour standing (optional)

150 ml/5 fl oz extra virgin olive oil
5 tbsp white wine vinegar
or lemon juice

1 garlic clove, finely chopped
pinch of sugar
2 tsp Dijon mustard
1 tbsp chopped fresh parsley
salt and pepper

1 Place all the ingredients into a screw-top jar and shake vigorously.

2 If there is time, set the jar aside at room temperature for 1 hour to allow the flavours to infuse.

3 Shake well again before using. The vinaigrette may be stored in the jar in the refrigerator for 2–3 days. Shake well before using.

thousand island dressing

makes: about 400 ml/14 fl oz
preparation time: 5 minutes

300 ml/10 fl oz good-quality mayonnaise
5 tbsp mild chilli sauce
2 tbsp tomato ketchup
2 spring onions, finely chopped
1 hard-boiled egg, shelled and chopped
2 gherkins, finely chopped
1 tsp Dijon mustard

1 Place all the ingredients in a bowl and whisk well to mix.

2 Cover tightly with clingfilm and chill in the refrigerator until required.

3 Stir the dressing again before serving chilled.

soups & starters

There is nothing quite so comforting and welcoming as home-made soup, but there is a common assumption that making it will somehow involve endless hours toiling over a bubbling pot in a steamy kitchen. Of course, some traditional soups do take a long time to cook and can involve lots of preparation, but there are others that are just as delicious and that can be made very quickly and easily. Within 20 minutes of getting home on a cold, dark night, you can serve a hungry family a satisfying tureen of Old English Cheese Soup (see page 26); in the same amount of time you can dish up a meal-in-a-bowl of Zuppa Pavese (see page 31) for a weekend lunch. With very little extra effort, you can impress your dinner party guests with Spicy Crab Soup (see page 33).

This chapter also features other fabulously fast starters for entertaining and for family meals. Start dinner with a taste of the exotic with little 'moneybags' filled with a mixture of pork and crabmeat – Thai Golden Pouches (see page 61) – or ever-popular Sesame Prawn Toasts (see page 54). A lavish platter of Antipasto Volente (see page 66) is the perfect choice for effortless entertaining and serving Scallops on Horseback (see page 46) with pre-dinner drinks will win hostess-of-the-year prizes. Set the mood for a long and lazy summer weekend lunch with Prosciutto & Figs (see page 74) or set the taste buds tingling with a sizzling plate of Vegetarian Fajitas (see page 71).

pumpkin soup

serves 4 **prep: 10 mins** ☾ **cook: 35–40 mins** ☺

This thick, creamy soup has a wonderful, warming golden colour.
It is flavoured with fresh orange and thyme leaves.

INGREDIENTS

2 tbsp olive oil

2 medium onions, chopped

2 garlic cloves, chopped

900 g/2 lb pumpkin, peeled and cut
into 2.5-cm/1-inch chunks

1.5 litres /2¾ pints boiling Vegetable
or Chicken Stock

finely grated rind and juice of 1 orange

3 tbsp fresh thyme leaves

salt and pepper

150 ml/5 fl oz milk

crusty bread, to serve

NUTRITIONAL INFORMATION

Calories 111

Protein 2g

Carbohydrate 5g

Sugars 4g

Fat 6g

Saturates 2g

---

variation

Try substituting a different fresh herb for
the thyme, such as chopped tarragon,
for a slightly different taste.

cook's tip

Pumpkins are usually large
vegetables. To make things a
little easier, ask the greengrocer
to cut a chunk off for you.
Alternatively, make double the
quantity and freeze the soup
for up to 3 months.

1 Heat the olive oil in a large saucepan. Add the onions to the pan and cook for 3–4 minutes, or until softened. Add the garlic and pumpkin and cook for a further 2 minutes, stirring well.

2 Add the boiling Stock, orange rind and juice and 2 tablespoons of the thyme to the saucepan. Leave to simmer, covered, for 20 minutes, or until the pumpkin is tender.

3 Place the mixture in a food processor and process until smooth. Alternatively, mash the mixture with a potato masher until smooth. Season to taste.

4 Return the soup to the saucepan and stir in the milk. Reheat for 3–4 minutes, or until piping hot but not boiling. Sprinkle with the remaining fresh thyme just before serving out.

5 Ladle the soup into 4 warmed soup bowls and serve with crusty bread.

calabrian mushroom soup

serves 4   **prep: 5 mins**   **cook: 25–30 mins**

The Calabrian Mountains in southern Italy provide wild mushrooms that give mushroom soup a rich flavour and colour.

INGREDIENTS

2 tbsp olive oil

1 onion, chopped

450 g/1 lb mixed mushrooms, such as
ceps, oyster and button mushrooms

300 ml/10 fl oz milk

850 ml/1½ pints hot Vegetable Stock
(see page 13)

salt and pepper

8 slices of rustic bread or French stick

2 garlic cloves, crushed

50 g/1¾ oz butter, melted

75 g/2¾ oz Gruyère cheese,
finely grated

NUTRITIONAL INFORMATION

Calories 452

Protein 15g

Carbohydrate 42g

Sugars 5g

Fat 26g

Saturates 12g

cook's tip

Mushrooms absorb liquid, which can lessen the flavour and affect cooking properties. Therefore, carefully wipe them with a damp cloth rather than rinsing them in water.

1 Preheat the grill to medium. Heat the oil in a large frying pan, add the onion and cook for 3–4 minutes, or until soft and golden.

2 Wipe each mushroom with a damp cloth and cut any large mushrooms into smaller, bite-sized pieces. Add the mushrooms to the pan, stirring quickly to coat them in the oil.

3 Add the milk to the pan, bring to the boil, cover and leave to simmer for about 5 minutes. Gradually stir in the hot Vegetable Stock and season with salt and pepper to taste.

4 Toast the bread on both sides under the preheated grill, until golden.

5 Mix the garlic and butter together. Spoon generously over the toast. Place the toast in the bottom of a large tureen or divide it among 4 individual serving bowls, then ladle over the hot soup. Top with the grated Gruyère cheese and serve at once.

tomato & pasta soup

cook: 50–55 mins   **prep: 5 mins**   **serves 4**

*Plum tomatoes are ideal for making soups and sauces
as they have denser, less watery flesh than rounder varieties.*

NUTRITIONAL INFORMATION	
Calories	503
Protein	9g
Carbohydrate	59g
Sugars	16g
Fat	28g
Saturates	17g

INGREDIENTS

55 g/2 oz unsalted butter

1 large onion, chopped

600 ml/1 pint Vegetable Stock
(see page 13)

900 g/2 lb Italian plum tomatoes,
skinned and roughly chopped

pinch of bicarbonate of soda

225 g/8 oz dried fusilli

salt and pepper

1 tbsp caster sugar

150 ml/5 fl oz double cream

fresh basil leaves, to garnish

variation

To make orange and
tomato soup, simply use
half the quantity of
Vegetable Stock topped
up with the same amount
of fresh orange juice.

1 Melt the butter in a large saucepan, add the onion and cook for 3 minutes, stirring. Add half of the Stock to the saucepan with the chopped tomatoes and bicarbonate of soda. Bring the soup to the boil, then reduce the heat and simmer for 20 minutes. Remove from the heat and set aside to cool.

2 Transfer the cooled soup to a food processor or blender and blend into a purée. Pour through a fine strainer back into the saucepan.

3 Add the remaining Vegetable Stock and the fusilli to the saucepan, and season to taste. Add the sugar to the saucepan, bring to the boil, then reduce the heat and simmer for 15 minutes.

4 Ladle the soup into a warmed tureen, swirl the double cream over the surface and garnish with fresh basil leaves. Serve immediately.

vegetable & bean soup

serves 4   **prep: 30 mins** ↺   **cook: 30 mins** ♨

This filling soup is made from a wonderful combination of cannellini beans, fresh vegetables and vermicelli, and is made even richer by the addition of pesto and dried porcini mushrooms.

INGREDIENTS

1 small aubergine	2 tsp dried basil
1 carrot	15 g/½ oz dried porcini mushrooms,
1 leek	soaked for 10 minutes in enough
2 large tomatoes	warm water to cover
1 potato, peeled	50 g/1¾ oz vermicelli
425 g/15 oz canned cannellini beans	3 tbsp shop-bought pesto
850 ml/1½ pints hot Vegetable or	freshly grated Parmesan cheese,
Chicken Stock (see page 13)	to serve (optional)

NUTRITIONAL INFORMATION

Calories	.294
Protein	.11g
Carbohydrate	.30g
Sugars	.2g
Fat	.16g
Saturates	.2g

variation

Bring a Mediterranean flavour to the soup by substituting the carrot, potato and leek with chopped courgette, diced pepper and chopped fried onion.

cook's tip

You can soften the aubergine slices before quartering them by placing them in a colander and sprinkling them with salt. Set aside for 20 minutes to draw out the juices, then rinse in cold water.

1 Slice the aubergine into rings about 1 cm/½ inch thick, then cut each ring into quarters. Cut the carrot into sticks about 2.5 cm/1 inch long and cut the leek into rings. Cut the tomatoes and potato into small dice.

2 Place the cannellini beans and their liquid in a large saucepan.

Add the aubergine, carrot, leek, tomatoes and potatoes, stirring to mix. Add the Stock to the saucepan and bring to the boil. Reduce the heat and leave to simmer for 15 minutes.

3 Add the basil, dried mushrooms and their soaking liquid and the vermicelli and simmer for

5 minutes, or until all of the vegetables are tender.

4 Remove the saucepan from the heat, stir in the pesto and serve with freshly grated Parmesan cheese, if using.

artichoke soup

serves 4

prep: 5 mins,
plus 3–4 hrs chilling

cook: 15 mins

This refreshing chilled soup is ideal for al fresco dining. Bear in mind that it needs to be chilled for 3–4 hours, so allow plenty of time.

INGREDIENTS

1 tbsp olive oil

1 onion, chopped

1 garlic clove, crushed

800 g/1 lb 12 oz canned artichoke hearts, drained

600 ml/1 pint hot Vegetable Stock (see page 13)

2 tbsp fresh thyme leaves

150 ml/5 fl oz single cream

2 sun-dried tomatoes, cut into strips, to garnish

crusty bread, to serve

NUTRITIONAL INFORMATION

Calories	159
Protein	2g
Carbohydrate	5g
Sugars	2g
Fat	15g
Saturates	6g

variation

Try adding 2 tablespoons of dry vermouth, such as Martini, to the soup in Step 3, if you wish.

1 Heat the oil in a large saucepan, add the onion and garlic and cook, stirring, for 2–3 minutes or until just softened.

2 Using a sharp knife, roughly chop the artichoke hearts. Add them to the saucepan. Pour in the hot Vegetable Stock, stirring well. Bring the mixture to the boil,

then reduce the heat and leave to simmer, covered, for about 3 minutes.

3 Transfer the soup into a food processor or blender and blend until smooth. Alternatively, push the mixture through a sieve to remove any lumps. Return the soup to the saucepan. Stir in the fresh thyme and single

cream. Transfer the soup into a large bowl and leave to cool, then cover and chill in the refrigerator for about 3–4 hours.

4 Ladle the soup into 4 bowls and garnish with strips of sun-dried tomato. Serve with fresh crusty bread.

spinach & mascarpone soup

⏱ **cook: 35 mins**   🕒 **prep: 5 mins**   **serves 4**

Spinach is the basis for this delicious soup, but use sorrel or watercress instead for a pleasant change.

NUTRITIONAL INFORMATION	
Calories	.537
Protein	.6g
Carbohydrate	.9g
Sugars	.2g
Fat	.53g
Saturates	.29g

INGREDIENTS

55 g/2 oz butter

1 bunch spring onions, trimmed and chopped

2 celery sticks, chopped

350 g/12 oz spinach

850 ml/1½ pints Vegetable Stock (see page 13)

225 g/8 oz mascarpone cheese

salt and pepper

1 tbsp olive oil

2 slices thick-cut bread, cut into cubes

½ tsp caraway seeds

sesame breadsticks, to serve

variation

Any leafy vegetable can be made into a soup following this recipe. Try sorrel, watercress, young beetroot leaves or lettuce instead of the spinach.

1 Melt half the butter in a large saucepan. Add the spring onions and celery and cook gently for about 5 minutes, or until softened.

2 Pack the spinach into the saucepan. Add the Vegetable Stock and bring to the boil, then reduce the heat and simmer, covered, for 15–20 minutes.

3 Transfer the soup to a food processor or blender and blend until smooth. Alternatively, pass the mixture through a sieve. Return the soup to the saucepan. Add the mascarpone cheese and cook over a low heat, stirring, until smooth and blended. Season with salt and pepper to taste.

4 Heat the remaining butter with the oil in a frying pan. Add the bread cubes and cook in the hot oil until golden brown. Add the caraway seeds towards the end of cooking, so that they do not burn.

5 Ladle the soup into 4 warmed bowls. Sprinkle the bread cubes over the top and serve immediately, accompanied by the sesame breadsticks.

cream of pea soup

serves 4 **prep: 10 mins** ⏲ **cook: 18 mins** ⏲

This attractive, pale green soup is subtly flavoured with mint and smoked salmon and would make a good first course for a dinner party. Serve with plenty of crusty bread, if you like.

INGREDIENTS

25 g/1 oz butter

1 onion, finely chopped

600 g/1 lb 5 oz frozen peas

700 ml/1¼ pints Chicken Stock (see page 13)

4 tbsp crème fraîche

115 g/4 oz smoked salmon, diced

2 tsp lemon juice

salt and pepper

2 fresh mint sprigs, leaves shredded

crusty bread, to serve

NUTRITIONAL INFORMATION

Calories	238
Protein	. . . . .17g
Carbohydrate	. . . . .18g
Sugars	. . . . .6g
Fat	. . . . .11g
Saturates	. . . . .6g

---

variation

Use the same amount of fresh ready-shelled peas instead of frozen and substitute the mint with 1–2 teaspoons chopped fresh tarragon.

---

cook's tip

Using a hand-held electric blender to purée the soup in Step 2 will save both time and washing up. If you do not have time to make the Chicken Stock, use a good-quality stock cube instead.

1 Melt the butter in a large, heavy-based saucepan. Add the onion and cook over a low heat, stirring occasionally, for 5 minutes, or until softened. Add the peas and Chicken Stock. Bring to the boil, cover and simmer gently for 10 minutes, or until the peas are tender.

2 Remove the saucepan from the heat and leave to cool slightly, then pour into a food processor and process until smooth. Alternatively, use a hand-held electric blender to purée the soup in the saucepan.

3 Return the soup to the saucepan, add the crème fraîche and return to a simmer. Stir in the smoked salmon and lemon juice and season to taste with salt and pepper. Sprinkle with the shredded mint, ladle into warmed soup bowls and serve immediately with crusty bread.

old english cheese soup

serves 4   **prep: 10 mins** ⏲   **cook: 10 mins** ⏲

Ready in a matter of minutes, this is a filling and heart-warming soup. Serve with crusty bread as an antidote to winter's chills.

INGREDIENTS

55 g/2 oz butter

55 g/2 oz plain flour

425 ml/15 fl oz Chicken Stock (see page 13)

300 ml/10 fl oz milk

2 carrots, grated

175 g/6 oz Cheddar cheese, grated

salt and pepper

crusty bread, to serve

NUTRITIONAL INFORMATION

Calories	390
Protein	15g
Carbohydrate	17g
Sugars	6g
Fat	30g
Saturates	19g

1 Melt the butter in a large, heavy-based saucepan. Sprinkle in the flour and cook, stirring constantly, for 1 minute. Remove the saucepan from the heat and gradually stir in the Chicken Stock and milk.

2 Return to the heat and bring to the boil, stirring constantly, then simmer for 3–4 minutes, or until the soup is thickened and smooth. Add the grated carrots and simmer for 3 minutes, then stir in the grated cheese.

3 When the cheese has melted, season to taste with salt and pepper. Ladle the soup into warmed soup bowls and serve immediately with crusty bread.

variation

If you like, you can serve this soup with a few garlic croûtons (see page 85, Step 2) sprinkled on top.

carrot & orange soup

cook: 20 mins   **prep: 10 mins**   serves 6

Colourful, delicious and laced with just a hint of sweetness, this classic soup can be served at any time of year.

NUTRITIONAL INFORMATION	
Calories	150
Protein	2g
Carbohydrate	19g
Sugars	13g
Fat	8g
Saturates	5g

INGREDIENTS

55 g/2 oz butter

2 onions, grated

salt and pepper

700 g/1 lb 9 oz carrots, grated

1 large potato, grated

2 tbsp grated orange rind

1.4–1.7 litres/2½–3 pints boiling water

juice of 1 large orange

2 tbsp chopped fresh parsley, to garnish

cook's tip

To save time, squeeze the orange and chop the fresh parsley while the soup is simmering in Step 2 and use a hand-held electric blender to purée the soup.

1 Melt the butter in a large, heavy-based saucepan. Add the onions and cook over a medium heat, stirring constantly, for 3 minutes. Sprinkle with a little salt, add the carrots and potato, then cover, reduce the heat and cook for 5 minutes.

2 Stir the orange rind into the saucepan, then add enough boiling water to cover. Return to the boil, cover and simmer briskly for 10 minutes. Add the orange juice.

3 Remove the saucepan from the heat and leave to cool slightly, then pour into a food processor and process until a smooth purée forms. Alternatively, use a hand-held electric blender to purée the soup in the saucepan. Return the soup to the saucepan, adding a little more boiling water if it is too thick. Return to the boil, taste and adjust the seasoning if necessary and ladle into warmed soup bowls. Garnish with chopped parsley and serve immediately.

tomato soup

serves 4   **prep: 10 mins**   **cook: 25 mins**

Soup made from fresh tomatoes is nothing like canned or packet soups and is destined to become a firm family favourite.

INGREDIENTS

55 g/2 oz butter

1 onion, finely chopped

700 g/1 lb 9 oz tomatoes, finely chopped

salt and pepper

600 ml/1 pint hot Chicken or Vegetable Stock (see page 13)

pinch of sugar

100 ml/3½ fl oz single cream

2 tbsp shredded fresh basil leaves

1 tbsp chopped fresh parsley

NUTRITIONAL INFORMATION

Calories	.200
Protein	.3g
Carbohydrate	.11g
Sugars	.10g
Fat	.17g
Saturates	.11g

variation

Replace the chopped fresh parsley with the same amount of snipped fresh chives and serve with freshly grated Parmesan cheese sprinkled on the top.

cook's tip

If you like, peel the tomatoes while the onion is cooking in Step 1. Cut a cross in the base of each tomato, place in a bowl and cover with boiling water. Leave for 1 minute, drain and peel off the skins.

1 Melt half the butter in a large, heavy-based saucepan. Add the onion and cook over a low heat, stirring occasionally, for 5 minutes, or until softened. Add the tomatoes, season to taste with salt and pepper and cook for 5 minutes.

2 Pour in the hot Chicken or Vegetable Stock, return to the boil, then reduce the heat and cook for 10 minutes.

3 Push the soup through a sieve with the back of a wooden spoon to remove the tomato skins and seeds. Return to the saucepan and stir in the sugar, cream, remaining butter, basil and parsley. Heat through briefly, but do not allow to boil. Ladle into warmed soup bowls and serve immediately.

mushroom soup

serves 4 **prep: 10 mins** ⏲ **cook: 15–18 mins** ⏲

This is a tasty soup when made with ordinary cultivated mushrooms, but for a special occasion you could make it with wild mushrooms for a more intense flavour.

INGREDIENTS

55 g/2 oz butter

1 onion, finely chopped

225 g/8 oz mushrooms, sliced

25 g/1 oz plain flour

425 ml/15 fl oz hot Chicken Stock
(see page 13)

150 ml/5 fl oz milk

salt and pepper

1 tbsp chopped fresh parsley, plus
extra to garnish

4 tbsp single cream

NUTRITIONAL INFORMATION

Calories	.200
Protein	.4g
Carbohydrate	.11g
Sugars	.5g
Fat	.16g
Saturates	.10g

cook's tip

If you like a chunkier soup, do not process to a purée, simply season to taste with salt and pepper and stir in the parsley and cream in Step 3.

1 Melt the butter in a large, heavy-based saucepan. Add the onion and cook over a low heat, stirring occasionally, for 5 minutes, or until softened. Add the mushrooms and cook for 5 minutes.

2 Sprinkle in the flour and cook, stirring constantly, for 1 minute. Remove the saucepan from the heat and gradually stir in the hot Chicken Stock. Return to the heat and bring to the boil, stirring constantly. Stir in the milk.

3 Pour the soup into a food processor and process to a smooth purée, then return to the saucepan. Heat through briefly, season to taste with salt and pepper and stir in the parsley and cream. Do not allow the soup to boil. Ladle into warmed soup bowls, garnish with chopped parsley and then serve immediately.

zuppa pavese

⏱ **cook: 10 mins**   ⏱ **prep: 10 mins**   **serves 4**

It is important to use a good-quality, clear beef stock or consommé for this unusual Italian soup. It would make a wonderful light lunch or an ideal first course for a dinner party.

NUTRITIONAL INFORMATION	
Calories 320	
Protein 15g	
Carbohydrate 17g	
Sugars 1g	
Fat 22g	
Saturates 12g	

INGREDIENTS

1 litre/1¾ pints clear Beef Stock

(see page 13)

or consommé

55 g/2 oz butter

4 slices white bread

55 g/2 oz freshly grated

Parmesan cheese

4 eggs

salt

variation

Poach the eggs. Bring a pan of water to the boil, then simmer. Break an egg into a cup, stir the water and slide in the egg. Cook for 3–4 minutes. Drain.

1 Pour the stock or consommé into a large, heavy-based saucepan and heat gently.

2 Meanwhile, melt the butter in a large, heavy-based frying pan. Add the bread and fry over a medium heat for 4–5 minutes, or until golden brown and crisp on both sides. Remove the fried bread from the frying pan, drain on kitchen paper, then place in the base of 4 large soup bowls.

3 Sprinkle two-thirds of the Parmesan cheese over the fried bread. Break 1 egg on to each slice of fried bread, season to taste with salt and sprinkle with the remaining grated Parmesan cheese. Very carefully ladle the hot stock or consommé into the soup bowls and serve immediately.

spicy crab soup

cook: 15 mins   **prep: 10 mins**   **serves 4**

NUTRITIONAL INFORMATION

Calories	95
Protein	. . . . .9g
Carbohydrate	. . . . .9g
Sugars	. . . . .2g
Fat	. . . . .3g
Saturates	. . . . .0g

variation

If Chinese rice wine is not available, then use the same amount of dry sherry instead and replace the rice vinegar with white wine vinegar.

Use only white crabmeat for this Chinese-style soup, as the brown meat will disintegrate. You can use fresh, frozen or canned crab.

INGREDIENTS

1 litre/1¾ pints Chicken Stock (see page 13)

2 tomatoes, peeled and finely chopped

2.5-cm/1-inch piece of fresh root ginger, finely chopped

1 small fresh red chilli, deseeded and finely chopped

2 tbsp Chinese rice wine

1 tbsp rice vinegar

¾ tsp sugar

1 tbsp cornflour

2 tbsp water

175 g/6 oz white crabmeat, thawed if frozen or drained if canned

salt and pepper

2 spring onions, shredded, to garnish

cook's tip

Chinese rice wine and rice vinegar are usually available from some large supermarkets as well as from Chinese food shops.

1 Pour the Chicken Stock into a large, heavy-based saucepan and add the tomatoes, ginger, chilli, rice wine, vinegar and sugar. Bring to the boil, then reduce the heat, cover and simmer for 10 minutes.

2 Mix the cornflour and water together in a small bowl until a smooth paste forms, then stir into the soup. Simmer, stirring constantly, for 2 minutes, or until slightly thickened.

3 Gently stir in the crabmeat and heat through for 2 minutes. Season to taste with salt and pepper, then ladle into warmed soup bowls and serve immediately, garnished with the shredded spring onions.

lamb & rice soup

serves 4 **prep: 5 mins** ⟲ **cook: 35 mins** ⟲

The addition of rice makes this a very filling and substantial soup, and the tender lamb and vegetables turn it into a full meal.

INGREDIENTS

150 g/5½ oz lean lamb

salt

50 g/1¾ oz rice

850 ml/1½ pints lamb stock

1 leek, sliced

1 garlic clove, thinly sliced

2 tsp light soy sauce

1 tsp rice wine vinegar

1 medium open-cap mushroom, thinly sliced

NUTRITIONAL INFORMATION

Calories 116

Protein 9g

Carbohydrate 12g

Sugars 0.2g

Fat 4g

Saturates 2g

variation

Use a few dried Chinese mushrooms, rehydrated as instructed on the packet and chopped, instead of the open-cap mushroom. Add in Step 4.

1 Using a sharp knife, trim any fat from the lamb and cut the meat into thin strips. Set aside until required.

2 Bring a large pan of lightly salted water to the boil and add the rice. Bring back to the boil, stir once, reduce the heat and cook for 10–15 minutes, until tender.

Drain the cooked rice, rinse under cold running water, drain again and set aside.

3 Put the lamb stock in a large saucepan and bring to the boil. Add the lamb strips, leek, garlic, soy sauce and rice wine vinegar, reduce the heat, cover and simmer for 10 minutes, or until the lamb is tender and cooked through.

4 Add the mushroom slices and cooked rice to the saucepan and cook for a further 2–3 minutes, or until the mushroom is completely cooked through.

5 Ladle the soup into 4 warmed bowls and serve immediately.

chunky potato & beef soup

cook: 35 mins   **prep: 5 mins**   **serves 4**

This is a real winter warmer – pieces of tender beef and chunky mixed vegetables are cooked in a liquor flavoured with sherry.

NUTRITIONAL INFORMATION

Calories	187
Protein	14g
Carbohydrate	12g
Sugars	3g
Fat	9g
Saturates	2g

INGREDIENTS

2 tbsp vegetable oil

225 g/8 oz lean braising or frying steak, cut into strips

225 g/8 oz new potatoes, halved

1 carrot, diced

2 celery sticks, sliced

2 leeks, sliced

850 ml/1½ pints Beef Stock (see page 13)

8 baby sweetcorn cobs, sliced

1 bouquet garni

2 tbsp dry sherry

salt and pepper

chopped fresh parsley, to garnish

crusty bread, to serve

cook's tip

Make double the quantity of soup and freeze the remainder in a rigid container for later use. When ready to use, leave in the refrigerator to defrost thoroughly, then heat until piping hot.

1 Heat the vegetable oil in a large saucepan. Add the strips of meat to the saucepan and cook for 3 minutes, turning constantly. Add the potatoes, carrot, celery and leeks to the saucepan. Cook for a further 5 minutes, stirring.

2 Pour the Beef Stock into the saucepan and bring to the boil. Reduce the heat until the liquid is simmering, then add the baby sweetcorn cobs and the bouquet garni. Cook for a further 20 minutes, or until cooked through.

3 Remove and discard the bouquet garni. Stir the dry sherry into the soup, then season to taste.

4 Ladle the soup into warmed bowls and garnish with the chopped fresh parsley. Serve at once with crusty bread.

mushroom & noodle soup

serves 4   **prep: 5 mins** ⟲   **cook: 10 mins** ⏱

A light, refreshing, clear soup of mushrooms, cucumber and small pieces of rice noodles, flavoured with soy sauce and a touch of garlic.

INGREDIENTS

125 g/4½ oz flat or   2 tbsp vegetable oil
open-cup mushrooms   600 ml/1 pint water
½ cucumber   25 g/1 oz Chinese rice noodles
2 spring onions   ¾ tsp salt
1 garlic clove   1 tbsp soy sauce

NUTRITIONAL INFORMATION

Calories 84

Protein 1g

Carbohydrate 3g

Sugars 1g

Fat 8g

Saturates 1g

variation

For a little extra spice, add a chopped fresh red chilli to the soup with the spring onions and garlic in Step 2.

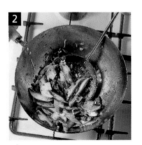

cook's tip

Scooping the seeds out from the cucumber gives it a prettier effect when sliced, and also helps to reduce any bitterness, but if you prefer, you can leave them in.

1 Wash the mushrooms and pat dry with kitchen paper. Slice thinly. Do not remove the peel, as this adds more flavour. Halve the cucumber lengthways. Scoop out the seeds using a teaspoon, then slice the flesh thinly. Chop the spring onions finely and cut the garlic clove into thin strips.

2 Heat the oil in a large saucepan or wok. Add the spring onions and garlic and stir-fry for 30 seconds. Add the mushrooms and stir-fry for 2–3 minutes.

3 Stir in the water. Break the noodles into short lengths and add to the soup. Bring to the boil, stirring.

4 Add the cucumber slices, salt and soy sauce, and simmer for 2–3 minutes.

5 Ladle the soup into warmed bowls, distributing the noodles and vegetables evenly.

chicken & leek soup

serves 4-6   **prep: 5 mins** ⏲   **cook: 1 hr 15 mins** ⏲

This fresh, satisfying soup, packed full of protein and fibre, is substantial enough to be served as a main course. If you like, you can add a touch of colour with some diced red pepper.

INGREDIENTS

25 g/1 oz butter

350 g/12 oz boneless chicken

350 g/12 oz leeks, cut into
2.5-cm/1-inch pieces

1.2 litres/2 pints Chicken Stock
(see page 13)

1 bouquet garni sachet

salt and white pepper

8 pitted prunes, halved

70 g/2¼ oz cooked rice

1 red pepper, diced (optional)

NUTRITIONAL INFORMATION

Calories	183
Protein	21g
Carbohydrate	4g
Sugars	4g
Fat	9g
Saturates	5g

variation

Instead of the bouquet garni sachet, you can use a bunch of fresh mixed herbs, tied together with string. Choose herbs such as parsley, thyme and rosemary.

1 Melt the butter in a large saucepan. Add the chicken and leeks and cook for 8 minutes.

2 Add the Chicken Stock and bouquet garni sachet to the saucepan and stir well, then season with salt and pepper to taste. Bring to the boil and simmer for 45 minutes.

3 Add the prunes to the saucepan with the cooked rice and diced pepper, if using, and simmer for about 20 minutes.

4 Remove the bouquet garni sachet from the soup and discard. Ladle into warmed soup bowls and serve immediately.

partan bree

cook: 35 mins   **prep: 1 hr**   **serves 6**

This traditional Scottish soup is based on fish stock, thickened with a delicious purée of rice and crab meat cooked in milk, and flavoured with citrus juice and anchovy essence.

NUTRITIONAL INFORMATION

Calories 112

Protein 7g

Carbohydrate 18g

Sugars 5g

Fat 2g

Saturates 0.3g

INGREDIENTS

1 medium-sized boiled crab

85 g/3 oz long-grain rice

600 ml/1 pint skimmed milk

salt and pepper

600 ml/1 pint fish stock

1 tbsp anchovy essence

2 tsp lime or lemon juice

1 tbsp chopped fresh parsley or l tsp chopped fresh thyme

3–4 tbsp soured cream (optional)

snipped chives, to garnish

cook's tip

If you are unable to buy a whole crab, use about 175 g/ 6 oz frozen crab meat and thaw thoroughly before use, or 175 g/6 oz canned crab meat, thoroughly drained.

1. Remove and reserve all the brown and white meat from the body of the crab. Crack the claws, remove and chop the meat and reserve.

2. Put the rice and milk in a saucepan and bring slowly to the boil. Cover and simmer gently for about 20 minutes.

3. Add the reserved brown and white meat from the body of the crab, season and simmer for a further 5 minutes. Leave the mixture to cool slightly, then transfer to a food processor or blender and blend until smooth. Alternatively, press the mixture through a sieve.

4. Pour the soup into a clean saucepan and add the fish stock and reserved claw meat. Bring slowly to the boil, then add the anchovy essence and lime juice and adjust the seasoning. Simmer for a further 2–3 minutes.

5. Stir in the herbs, then ladle into warmed soup bowls. Swirl a little soured cream through each serving, if using. Garnish with snipped chives and serve.

spicy dahl & carrot soup

serves 6   **prep: 10 mins**   **cook: 50 mins**

This delicious, warming and nutritious soup includes a selection of spices to give it a 'kick'. It is simple to make and extremely good to eat.

INGREDIENTS

125 g/4½ oz split red lentils	1 tsp ground coriander
1.2 litres/2 pints Vegetable Stock	1 fresh green chilli, deseeded
(see page 13)	and chopped
350 g/12 oz carrots, sliced	½ tsp ground turmeric
2 onions, chopped	1 tbsp lemon juice
250 g/9 oz canned chopped tomatoes	salt
2 garlic cloves, chopped	300 ml/10 fl oz skimmed milk
2 tbsp vegetable ghee or oil	2 tbsp chopped fresh coriander
1 tsp ground cumin	natural yogurt, to serve

NUTRITIONAL INFORMATION

Calories 173

Protein 9g

Carbohydrate 24g

Sugars 11g

Fat 5g

Saturates 1g

variation

If you can't find a fresh green chilli, you can substitute 1 teaspoon of minced chilli from a jar.

cook's tip

Make double the quantity of soup and freeze the remainder in a rigid container for later use. When ready to use, leave in the refridgerator to defrost thoroughly, then heat until piping hot.

1 Place the lentils in a sieve and wash well under cold running water. Drain and place in a large saucepan with 850 ml/1½ pints of the vegetable stock, the carrots, onions, tomatoes and garlic. Bring the mixture to the boil, then reduce the heat, cover and simmer for 30 minutes.

2 Meanwhile, heat the ghee in a small saucepan, add the cumin, coriander, chilli and turmeric and cook gently for 1 minute. Remove from the heat and stir in the lemon juice and salt to taste.

3 Purée the soup in batches in a food processor or blender. Return the soup to the saucepan, add the spice mixture and the remaining Stock and simmer for 10 minutes.

4 Add the milk to the soup and adjust the seasoning according to taste. Stir in the chopped coriander and reheat gently. Serve hot, with a swirl of natural yogurt.

red lentil soup with yogurt

serves 4   **prep: 5 mins** ⟳   **cook: 30 mins** ⟳

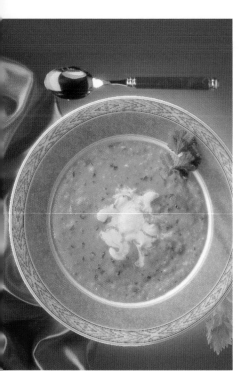

This tasty red lentil soup, made in the microwave, is delicately flavoured with chopped coriander. The yogurt adds a light piquancy.

INGREDIENTS

25 g/1 oz butter

1 onion, chopped finely

1 celery stick, chopped finely

1 large carrot, grated

1 dried bay leaf

225 g/8 oz red lentils

1.2 litres/2 pints hot Vegetable or
Chicken Stock (see page 13)

salt and pepper

2 tbsp chopped fresh coriander

4 tbsp low-fat natural yogurt

fresh coriander sprigs, to garnish

NUTRITIONAL INFORMATION

Calories	.280
Protein	.17g
Carbohydrate	.40g
Sugars	.6g
Fat	.7g
Saturates	.4g

cook's tip

For an extra creamy soup try adding low-fat crème fraîche or soured cream instead of the yogurt in Step 4.

1 Place the butter, onion and celery in a large bowl. Cover and cook on High power for 3 minutes.

2 Add the carrot, bay leaf and lentils. Pour over the Stock. Cover and cook on High power for 15 minutes, stirring halfway through. Remove from the microwave, cover and leave to stand for

5 minutes. Remove the bay leaf, then transfer in batches to a food processor or blender and blend until smooth. Alternatively, press the mixture through a sieve.

3 Pour into a clean bowl. Season to taste and stir in the coriander. Cover and cook on High power for 4–5 minutes, until piping hot.

4 Ladle into warmed bowls. Stir 1 tablespoon of yogurt into each serving and garnish with sprigs of fresh coriander.

yogurt & spinach soup

🕒 **cook: 30 mins**   ⏱ **prep: 15 mins**   **serves 4**

Whole young spinach leaves add vibrant colour to this unusual soup.
Serve with hot, crusty bread for a nutritious light meal.

NUTRITIONAL INFORMATION

Calories	.227
Protein	.14g
Carbohydrate	.29g
Sugars	.13g
Fat	.7g
Saturates	.2g

INGREDIENTS

600 ml/1 pint Chicken Stock
(see page 13)
salt and pepper
55 g/2 oz long-grain rice,
rinsed and drained
4 tbsp water
1 tbsp cornflour
600 ml/1 pint low-fat
natural yogurt
3 egg yolks, lightly beaten
juice of 1 lemon
350 g/12 oz young spinach leaves,
washed and drained
crusty bread, to serve

variation

You can substitute
watercress for the spinach
if you prefer, but cut off
any tough stalks and use
only the tender leaves.

1 Pour the Stock into a saucepan, season and bring to the boil. Add the rice and simmer for 10 minutes, until barely cooked. Remove from the heat.

2 Combine the water and cornflour to make a smooth paste.

3 Pour the yogurt into a separate saucepan and stir in the cornflour paste. Set over a low heat and bring slowly to the boil, stirring with a wooden spoon in one direction only. This prevents the yogurt from curdling on contact with the hot stock. When it has reached boiling point, stand the saucepan on a heat diffuser and leave to simmer gently for 10 minutes. Remove from the heat and allow to cool slightly, then stir in the egg yolks.

4 Pour the yogurt mixture into the stock, add the lemon juice and stir to blend thoroughly. Keep warm, but do not allow to boil.

5 Blanch the spinach in a saucepan of lightly salted boiling water for 2–3 minutes, until softened but not wilted. Drain well, then stir into the soup. Let the spinach warm through. Taste the soup and adjust the seasoning, if necessary. Serve in wide, shallow soup plates, with hot, fresh crusty bread.

thick onion soup

serves 6   **prep: 20 mins**   **cook: 1 hr 10 mins**

This delicious, creamy soup is made with grated carrot and parsley to give extra texture and colour. Serve with crusty cheese scones to turn it into a hearty lunch.

INGREDIENTS

75 g/2¾ oz butter	4–6 tbsp double cream
500 g/1 lb 2 oz onions, finely chopped	2 tbsp chopped fresh parsley,
1 garlic clove, crushed	to garnish
40 g/1½ oz plain flour	
600 ml/1 pint Vegetable Stock	**CHEESE SCONES**
(see page 13)	225 g/8 oz malted wheat or
600 ml/1 pint milk	wholemeal flour
salt and pepper	2 tsp baking powder
2 tsp lemon or lime juice	55 g/2 oz butter
good pinch of ground mixed spice	4 tbsp freshly grated Parmesan cheese
1 bay leaf	1 egg, beaten
1 carrot, roughly grated	about 75 ml/2½ fl oz milk

NUTRITIONAL INFORMATION

Calories	.277
Protein	.6g
Carbohydrate	.19g
Sugars	.12g
Fat	.20g
Saturates	.8g

variation

Knead 1 tablespoon of finely snipped fresh chives into the cheese scone dough at the end of Step 2.

cook's tip

Keep a little extra lemon or lime juice to hand in case you want to add more flavour to the soup before serving. Stir it in just before adding the cream in Step 4.

1 Melt the butter in a saucepan, add the onions and garlic and cook over a low heat, stirring frequently, for 10–15 minutes, until softened but not coloured. Add the flour and cook, stirring, for 1 minute, then gradually stir in the Stock and bring to the boil, stirring frequently. Add the milk, then bring the mixture back to the boil. Season to taste with salt and pepper and add the lemon juice, mixed spice and bay leaf. Cover and simmer for 25 minutes, or until the vegetables are tender. Discard the bay leaf.

2 Meanwhile, make the scones. Combine the flour, baking powder and seasoning and rub in the butter until the mixture resembles fine breadcrumbs. Stir in 3 tablespoons of the cheese, the egg and enough milk to mix to a soft dough.

3 Shape the dough into a bar about 2 cm/¾ inch thick. Place on a floured baking tray and mark into slices. Sprinkle with the remaining cheese and bake in a preheated oven, 220°C/425°F/Gas Mark 7, for about 20 minutes, until risen and golden brown.

4 Stir the carrot into the soup and simmer for 2–3 minutes. Add more lemon juice, if necessary. Stir in the cream and reheat. Garnish with chopped parsley and serve with the warm scones.

scallops on horseback

serves 4   **prep: 5 mins**   **cook: 10 mins**

These tasty little morsels would make wonderful hot canapés to serve at a dinner party with pre-dinner drinks.

INGREDIENTS

20 prepared scallops, thawed if frozen

2–3 tbsp lemon juice

salt and pepper

20 rindless streaky bacon rashers

tartare sauce, to serve

NUTRITIONAL INFORMATION	
Calories	.485
Protein	.53g
Carbohydrate	.4g
Sugars	.0g
Fat	.29g
Saturates	.10g

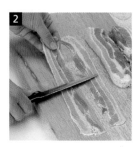

cook's tip

For a speedy tartare sauce, stir 2 tablespoons each chopped gherkins and capers into 300 ml/10 fl oz ready-made mayonnaise. Stir in snipped chives or finely chopped spring onions to taste and serve.

1 Preheat the grill to medium. Sprinkle the scallops with lemon juice and season to taste with salt and pepper.

2 Stretch the bacon with a flat-bladed knife, then wrap a rasher around each scallop, securing it with a wooden cocktail stick.

3 Cook under the preheated grill for 5 minutes on each side, or until cooked through. Serve immediately with tartare sauce.

pan-fried scallops & prawns

cook: 4 mins   **prep: 10 mins**   **serves 4**

As most shellfish needs very little cooking, it is the perfect choice for the cook in a hurry. It also looks attractive and tastes wonderful.

NUTRITIONAL INFORMATION

Calories 225

Protein 24g

Carbohydrate 11g

Sugars 0g

Fat 10g

Saturates 2g

INGREDIENTS

12 prepared scallops, thawed if frozen

12 large raw prawns, peeled
and deveined

salt and pepper

2 tbsp plain flour

3 tbsp olive oil

2 garlic cloves, finely chopped

2 tbsp chopped fresh parsley

3 tbsp lemon juice

cook's tip

If using frozen scallops, thaw out slowly in the refrigerator. Once they are completely thawed out, use immediately, or keep in the refrigerator until ready to cook but use on the same day.

1 Using a sharp knife, cut the scallops in half, then season the scallops and prawns with salt and pepper to taste. Spread the flour out on a plate and use to dust the scallops and prawns, shaking off the excess.

2 Heat the olive oil in a large, heavy-based frying pan. Add the floured scallops and prawns and cook over a medium heat for 2 minutes. Add the chopped garlic and parsley, then stir well, tossing the shellfish to coat, and cook, shaking the

frying pan occasionally, for 2 minutes, or until the scallops are opaque and the prawns have changed colour.

3 Add the lemon juice and toss well to coat. Transfer to warmed plates and serve immediately.

pepper salad

serves 4　　　　**prep: 5–10 mins**　　　　**cook: 35 mins**

Colourful marinated Mediterranean vegetables make a tasty starter, especially when served with fresh bread or Tomato Toasts.

INGREDIENTS

1 onion

2 red peppers

2 yellow peppers

3 tbsp olive oil

2 large courgettes, sliced

2 garlic cloves, sliced

1 tbsp balsamic vinegar

50 g/1¾ oz anchovy fillets, chopped

25 g/1 oz black olives, halved and stoned

salt and pepper

1 tbsp chopped fresh basil

TOMATO TOASTS

small stick of French bread

1 garlic clove, crushed

1 tomato, peeled and chopped

2 tbsp olive oil

salt and pepper

NUTRITIONAL INFORMATION

Calories 234

Protein 6g

Carbohydrate 15g

Sugars 4g

Fat 17g

Saturates 2g

variation

If you like, chop an aubergine into chunks, sprinkle with salt to draw out the juices, then rinse and add in Step 2 with an extra tablespoonful of oil.

cook's tip

If you find canned anchovies rather too salty, soak them in a saucer of cold milk for 5 minutes, then drain and pat dry with kitchen paper before using. The milk absorbs the salt.

1 Cut the onion into wedges. Core and deseed the peppers and cut into thick slices.

2 Heat the oil in a heavy-based frying pan. Add the onion, peppers, courgettes and garlic and cook gently for 20 minutes, stirring occasionally.

3 Add the vinegar, anchovies, olives and seasoning to taste, mix thoroughly and leave to cool. Spoon the cooled mixture on to individual plates and sprinkle with the basil.

4 To make the Tomato Toasts, preheat the oven to 220°C/425°F/Gas Mark 7. Cut the French bread diagonally into 1-cm/½-inch slices. Mix the garlic, tomato, oil and seasoning together, and spread thinly over each slice of bread.

5 Place the bread on a baking tray and bake in the preheated oven for 5–10 minutes, until crisp. Serve with the vegetable salad.

flambéed prawns

serves 4   **prep: 10 mins**   **cook: 20 mins**

Serve these fabulous hot prawns with a small portion of colourful salad leaves, such as oakleaf lettuce, radicchio or lollo rosso.

INGREDIENTS

40 g/1½ oz butter

2 shallots, chopped

225 g/8 oz cooked peeled prawns

115 g/4 oz button mushrooms, halved

1 tbsp lemon juice

pinch of freshly grated nutmeg

salt and pepper

3 tbsp brandy

150 ml/5 fl oz double cream

fresh flat-leaved parsley sprigs,
to garnish

mixed salad leaves, to serve

NUTRITIONAL INFORMATION

Calories	335
Protein	. . . . .14g
Carbohydrate	. . . . .2g
Sugars	. . . . .2g
Fat	. . . . .27g
Saturates	. . . . .17g

variation

You could use raw prawns rather than cooked. Add them in Step 1 with the mushrooms and cook for 5 minutes, or until they have changed colour.

1 Melt the butter in a large, heavy-based frying pan. Add the shallots and cook over a low heat, stirring occasionally, for 5 minutes. Add the prawns and mushrooms and cook, stirring occasionally, for 3–4 minutes, then season to taste with lemon juice, nutmeg, salt and pepper.

2 Measure the brandy into a metal ladle and warm over a very low heat. Ignite and pour the flaming brandy over the prawn mixture. Shake the frying pan gently until the flames have died down, then cook for a further 2–3 minutes.

3 Stir in the cream, increase the heat and cook, stirring constantly, until thickened. Divide between warmed serving plates, garnish with the parsley sprigs and serve immediately with mixed salad leaves.

tagliarini with gorgonzola

⏱ **cook: 20 mins**   ⏱ **prep: 5 mins**   **serves 4**

This simple, creamy pasta sauce is a classic Italian recipe. You could
use Danish blue cheese instead of the Gorgonzola, if you prefer.

NUTRITIONAL INFORMATION	
Calories	904
Protein	27g
Carbohydrate	83g
Sugars	4g
Fat	53g
Saturates	36g

INGREDIENTS

25 g/1 oz butter

225 g/8 oz Gorgonzola cheese,
roughly crumbled

150 ml/5 fl oz double cream

2 tbsp dry white wine

1 tsp cornflour

4 fresh sage sprigs, finely chopped

salt and white pepper

400 g/14 oz dried tagliarini

2 tbsp olive oil

cook's tip

When buying Gorgonzola,
always check that it is
creamy yellow with delicate
green veining. Avoid hard or
discoloured cheese. It should
have a rich, piquant aroma,
not a bitter smell.

1 Melt the butter in a heavy-based saucepan. Stir in 175 g/6 oz of the cheese and melt, over a low heat, for about 2 minutes.

2 Add the cream, white wine and cornflour and beat with a whisk until fully incorporated.

3 Stir in the sage and season to taste with salt and white pepper. Bring to the boil over a low heat, whisking constantly, until the sauce thickens. Remove from the heat and set aside while you cook the pasta.

4 Bring a large saucepan of lightly salted water to the boil. Add the tagliarini and 1 tablespoon of the olive oil. Cook the pasta for 8–10 minutes, or until just tender, then drain thoroughly and toss in the remaining olive oil. Transfer the pasta to a serving dish and keep warm.

5 Reheat the Gorgonzola sauce over a low heat, whisking constantly. Spoon the sauce over the tagliarini, generously sprinkle over the remaining cheese and serve.

smoked trout with pears

cook: 0 mins　　　　**prep: 10 mins**　　　　**serves 4**

NUTRITIONAL INFORMATION

Calories 329

Protein 37g

Carbohydrate 11g

Sugars 10g

Fat 16g

Saturates 4g

variation

Replace the horseradish with mustard
mayonnaise. Mix 3 teaspoons mustard,
2 teaspoons chopped fresh dill and
150 ml/5 fl oz mayonnaise. Season.

*Trout is hot-smoked, so needs no further cooking – a boon when
you are short of time. The fillets should be a delicate beige-pink
colour. Avoid darker ones, which will have been artificially coloured.*

INGREDIENTS

55 g/2 oz watercress

1 head of radicchio, torn into pieces

4 smoked trout fillets, skinned

2 ripe pears, such as Williams

2 tbsp lemon juice

2 tbsp extra virgin olive oil

salt and pepper

3 tbsp soured cream

2 tsp creamed horseradish

thinly sliced buttered brown bread,
crusts removed, to serve

cook's tip

Olive oil is very versatile as it
can be used for frying, cooking
and salad dressings. Use the
best-quality extra virgin olive oil
that you can find in dressings
and use the ordinary virgin
olive oil in cooking.

1 Place the watercress
and radicchio in a bowl.
Cut the trout fillets into thin
strips and add to the bowl.
Halve and core the pears, then
slice thinly. Place in a separate
bowl, add 4 teaspoons of the
lemon juice and toss to coat.
Add the pears to the salad.

2 To make the dressing,
mix the remaining
lemon juice and the olive oil
together in a bowl, then
season to taste with salt and
pepper. Pour the dressing over
the salad and toss well.
Transfer to a large salad bowl.

3 Mix the soured cream
and horseradish
together in a separate bowl
until thoroughly blended, then
spoon over the salad. Serve
with buttered brown bread.

sesame prawn toasts

serves 4 | **prep: 10 mins** ⟲ | **cook: 4–6 mins** 🝢

One of the most popular Chinese starters, these crisp, golden and succulent little toasts take only a few minutes to prepare.

INGREDIENTS

225 g/8 oz raw prawns, peeled and deveined

25 g/1 oz lard

1 egg white, lightly beaten

1 tsp chopped spring onions

½ tsp finely chopped fresh root ginger

1 tbsp Chinese rice wine or dry sherry

1 tsp cornflour

2 tsp water

salt and pepper

6 slices white bread, crusts removed

140 g/5 oz sesame seeds

groundnut oil, for deep-frying

NUTRITIONAL INFORMATION

Calories	445
Protein	. . . . .15g
Carbohydrate	. . . . .23g
Sugars	. . . . .1g
Fat	. . . . .33g
Saturates	. . . . .7g

---

variation

If you cannot find groundnut oil for deep-frying, then use vegetable or sunflower oil instead.

---

cook's tip

If you are using a wok, preheat it first without any oil until hot. This prevents the food sticking and ensures an even distribution of heat while cooking.

1 Place the prawns and lard on a chopping board and chop them together until they form a paste. Scrape into a bowl and stir in the egg white, spring onions, ginger and rice wine. Mix the cornflour and water together in a small bowl until a smooth paste forms, then stir into the prawn mixture and season to taste with salt and pepper.

2 Spread the prawn paste evenly over one side of each slice of bread. Spread out the sesame seeds on a flat plate or tray and gently press the spread side of each slice of bread into the seeds to coat.

3 Heat the groundnut oil in a preheated wok or large frying pan. Add half the slices of bread, spread-side down, and cook for 2–3 minutes, or until golden brown. Remove with a slotted spoon and drain on kitchen paper. Cook the remaining slices in the same way. Cut each slice into fingers and serve immediately.

chinese omelette

serves 4　　　　**prep: 5 mins** ☾　　　　**cook: 5 mins** ⏲

This is a fairly filling omelette, as it contains chicken and prawns.
It is cooked as a whole omelette, then sliced for serving.

INGREDIENTS

8 eggs

225 g/8 oz cooked chicken, shredded

12 raw tiger prawns, peeled
and deveined

2 tbsp snipped fresh chives

2 tsp light soy sauce

dash of chilli sauce

2 tbsp vegetable oil

NUTRITIONAL INFORMATION

Calories 309

Protein 34g

Carbohydrate 0.2g

Sugars 0g

Fat 19g

Saturates 5g

variation

Add extra flavour by
stirring in 3 tablespoons
of finely chopped fresh
coriander or 1 teaspoon
of sesame seeds with the
chives in Step 2.

1 Lightly beat the eggs in a large mixing bowl. Add the shredded chicken and tiger prawns to the eggs and mix well.

2 Stir in the chopped chives, soy sauce and chilli sauce, mixing well to combine all the ingredients.

3 Preheat a large frying pan over a medium heat. Add the vegetable oil. When the oil is hot, add the egg mixture to the pan, tilting the pan to coat the base completely. Cook over a medium heat, gently stirring the omelette with a fork, until the surface is just set and the underside is golden brown.

4 When the omelette is set, slide it out of the pan using a palette knife.

5 Cut the Chinese omelette into squares or slices and serve immediately. Alternatively, serve the omelette as a main course for two people.

crispy seaweed

⏱ **cook: 5 mins**   ⏱ **prep: 10 mins**   **serves 4**

This tasty Chinese starter is not all that it seems – the 'seaweed' is in fact pak choi which is fried, salted and tossed with pine kernels.

NUTRITIONAL INFORMATION

Calories 214

Protein 6g

Carbohydrate 15g

Sugars 14g

Fat 15g

Saturates 2g

INGREDIENTS

1 kg/2 lb 4 oz pak choi

about 850 ml/1½ pints groundnut oil

1 tsp salt

1 tbsp caster sugar

50 g/1¾ oz toasted pine kernels

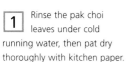

cook's tip

The tough, outer leaves of pak choi are discarded as these will spoil the overall taste and texture of the dish. Use savoy cabbage instead of pak choi if it is unavailable.

1 Rinse the pak choi leaves under cold running water, then pat dry thoroughly with kitchen paper.

2 Discarding any tough outer leaves, roll each pak choi leaf up, then slice thinly so that the leaves are finely shredded. Alternatively, use a food processor to shred the pak choi.

3 Heat the groundnut oil in a large wok or heavy-based frying pan. Carefully add the shredded pak choi and cook for 30 seconds, or until it shrivels up and becomes crispy. (You will probably need to do this in several batches.) Remove the crispy seaweed from the wok with a strainer and drain on kitchen paper.

4 Transfer the crispy seaweed to a large bowl, toss with the salt, sugar and pine kernels and serve.

spicy sweetcorn fritters

serves 4 | **prep: 5 mins** | **cook: 15 mins**

*Polenta can be found in most supermarkets or health food shops –
it is yellow in colour. It acts as a binding agent in this recipe.*

INGREDIENTS

225 g/8 oz canned or
frozen sweetcorn

2 fresh red chillies, deseeded and
very finely chopped

2 cloves garlic, crushed

10 kaffir lime leaves, very
finely chopped

2 tbsp chopped fresh coriander

1 large egg

75 g/2¾ oz polenta

100 g/3½ oz fine green beans,
very finely sliced

groundnut oil, for frying

NUTRITIONAL INFORMATION

Calories	.213
Protein	.5g
Carbohydrate	.30g
Sugars	.6g
Fat	.8g
Saturates	.1g

variation

Add 1 tablespoon of Satay Sauce
(see page 64) to the mixture in Step 1
for a slightly nuttier flavour.

cook's tip

Kaffir lime leaves are dark
green, glossy leaves that have a
lemony-lime flavour. They can
be bought from specialist Asian
stores either fresh or dried.
Fresh leaves impart the most
delicious flavour.

1 Place the sweetcorn,
chillies, garlic, lime
leaves, coriander, egg and
polenta in a large mixing bowl
and stir with a wooden spoon
to combine. Add the green
beans and mix well.

2 Divide the mixture into
small, evenly sized balls.

Flatten the balls of mixture
between the palms of your
hands to form rounds.

3 Heat a little groundnut
oil in a preheated wok
or large frying pan until very
hot. Cook the fritters in the
hot oil, in batches, until brown
and crispy on the outside,

turning occasionally. Leave
each batch of fritters to
drain on kitchen paper while
cooking the remainder.

4 Transfer the fritters to
warmed serving plates
and serve immediately.

thai golden pouches

cook: 10–15 mins　　　　**prep: 10 mins**　　　　**serves 4**

variation

If you cannot find the Thai chilli sauce, then use Tabasco or light soy sauce instead. Use groundnut or vegetable oil for deep-frying the pouches.

These crisp little 'moneybags' are totally irresistible. Serve them as a starter or as canapés with pre-dinner drinks.

INGREDIENTS

115 g/4 oz crabmeat, thawed if frozen or drained if canned

115 g/4 oz fresh pork mince

55 g/2 oz fresh shiitake mushrooms, finely chopped

1 tsp chopped fresh garlic

2 tbsp chopped spring onions

1 tbsp chopped fresh coriander

1 egg, lightly beaten

1 tbsp Thai fish sauce

1 tbsp dark soy sauce

pinch of sugar

pepper

20 wonton wrappers

oil, for deep-frying

Thai chilli sauce, to serve

cook's tip

Wonton wrappers are paper-thin squares of dough made from flour and egg. They are available from supermarkets and Chinese food shops. Thai chilli sauce is also available from Chinese food shops.

1 Mix the crabmeat, pork, mushrooms, garlic, spring onions, coriander, egg, fish sauce, soy sauce and sugar together in a bowl and season to taste with pepper.

2 Place 1 teaspoon of the mixture in the centre of a wonton wrapper. Fold up the edges and pinch the top together to seal. Fill the remaining wrappers in the same way.

3 Heat the oil in a preheated wok or large, heavy-based frying pan. Add the wontons, in batches, and deep-fry until golden brown and crisp. Remove with a slotted spoon and drain on kitchen paper. Serve immediately with Thai chilli sauce for dipping.

bruschetta

serves 4   **prep: 10 mins** ⏱   **cook: 15 mins** ⏱

These tasty little tomato and mozzarella cheese toasts can be served as finger food at a party and also as a starter. Remember to switch on the grill and oven to preheat before you start the preparation.

INGREDIENTS

2 small ciabatta loaves
175 ml/6 fl oz sun-dried tomato paste
280 g/10 oz mozzarella cheese, diced
1 tbsp chopped fresh oregano
pepper
2 tbsp olive oil
mixed salad leaves, to serve

NUTRITIONAL INFORMATION

Calories 578

Protein 24g

Carbohydrate 38g

Sugars 2g

Fat 37g

Saturates 12g

variation

If you cannot find fresh oregano, then use dried instead. Alternatively, use the same amount of chopped fresh basil.

1 Preheat the oven to 220°C/425°F/Gas Mark 7 and preheat the grill to medium. Slice the bread diagonally, discarding the end crusts, to give a total of about 24 slices. Toast the bread lightly on both sides under the preheated grill.

2 Spread the tomato paste evenly on to 1 side of each slice of toast, then top each with the diced mozzarella cheese.

3 Place the bruschetta on a large baking sheet and sprinkle with the oregano. Season to taste with pepper and drizzle with the olive oil. Bake in the preheated oven for 5 minutes, or until the mozzarella has melted. Leave to stand for 2 minutes, then serve warm with mixed salad leaves.

bacon with lamb's lettuce

cook: 10 mins   **prep: 10 mins**   **serves 6**

Lamb's lettuce, also known as corn salad and mâche, although it is neither true lettuce nor corn, has a sweet flavour that is perfectly complemented by crispy bacon and garlic croûtons.

NUTRITIONAL INFORMATION

Calories	270
Protein	8g
Carbohydrate	9g
Sugars	1g
Fat	23g
Saturates	5g

INGREDIENTS

6–8 tbsp sunflower oil

225 g/8 oz rindless streaky bacon, diced

2 garlic cloves, finely chopped

4 slices of white bread, crusts removed, cut into 1-cm/½-inch cubes

5 tbsp red wine vinegar

1 tbsp balsamic vinegar

2 tsp wholegrain mustard

salt and pepper

225 g/8 oz lamb's lettuce

cook's tip

If you buy lamb's lettuce with the root still attached, leave it to stand in a bowl of iced water for 1 hour to refresh (if you have time).

1 Heat 2 teaspoons of the sunflower oil in a large, heavy-based frying pan. Add the bacon and cook over a medium heat, stirring frequently, for 5 minutes, or until crisp. Remove from the frying pan with a slotted spoon and drain on kitchen paper. Add the garlic and diced bread to the frying pan and cook, stirring and tossing frequently, until crisp and golden brown on all sides. Remove from the frying pan with a slotted spoon and drain on kitchen paper.

2 Place the red wine vinegar, balsamic vinegar, mustard and remaining sunflower oil in a screw-top jar and shake vigorously, then pour into a bowl. Alternatively, mix the vinegars and mustard together in a bowl and whisk in the oil until the dressing is creamy. Season to taste with salt and pepper.

3 Add the lamb's lettuce and bacon to the dressing and toss to coat. Divide the salad between serving plates, sprinkle with the croûtons and serve.

chicken or beef satay

serves 6 **prep: 15 mins, plus 2 hrs marinating** **cook: 15 mins**

In this dish, strips of chicken or beef are threaded on to skewers, grilled and served with a rich, spicy peanut sauce.

INGREDIENTS

4 boneless, skinned chicken breasts or
750 g/1 lb 10 oz rump steak, trimmed

MARINADE

1 small onion, finely chopped
1 garlic clove, crushed
2.5-cm/1-inch piece fresh
root ginger, grated
2 tbsp dark soy sauce
2 tsp chilli powder
1 tsp ground coriander
2 tsp dark brown sugar
1 tbsp lemon or lime juice
1 tbsp vegetable oil

SATAY SAUCE

300 ml/10 fl oz coconut milk
4 tbsp crunchy peanut butter
1 tbsp nam pla (Thai fish sauce)
1 tsp lemon or lime juice
salt and pepper

NUTRITIONAL INFORMATION	
Calories	.314
Protein	.32g
Carbohydrate	.10g
Sugars	.8g
Fat	.16g
Saturates	.4g

variation

If you don't want to make the Satay Sauce yourself, try a shop-bought version – many supermarkets sell good, ready-made dipping sauces.

cook's tip

If you don't have any bamboo skewers, thin wooden skewers will work just as well. Soak them in cold water to prevent them from burning while the meat is cooking.

1 Place 18 bamboo skewers in cold water to soak. Using a sharp knife, trim any fat from the meat, then cut it into thin strips, about 7 cm/3 inches long.

2 To make the marinade, place all the ingredients in a shallow dish and mix well. Add the meat strips and turn in the marinade until well coated. Cover with clingfilm and leave in the refrigerator to marinate for 2 hours, or preferably overnight.

3 Preheat the grill to medium. Remove the meat from the marinade and thread it, concertina style, on to the pre-soaked skewers.

4 Grill the meat satays for 8–10 minutes, turning and brushing occasionally with the marinade, until completely cooked through.

5 Meanwhile, to make the sauce, mix the coconut milk with the peanut butter, nam pla and lemon juice in a saucepan. Bring to the boil and cook for 3 minutes. Season to taste. Transfer the sauce to a serving bowl and serve with the cooked satays.

antipasto volente

serves 6   **prep: 15 mins** ⏲   **cook: 0 mins** ⏲

In Italy, antipasti are served as starters before the pasta course.
The title of this dish translates roughly as 'take your pick'.

INGREDIENTS

200 g/7 oz canned tuna in oil, drained and flaked into chunks

115 g/4 oz canned sardines in oil, drained

100 g/3½ oz canned anchovy fillets in oil, drained

175 g/6 oz cooked peeled prawns, deveined

115 g/4 oz prosciutto, cut into strips

175 g/6 oz mozzarella cheese, sliced

390 g/13½ oz canned artichoke hearts, drained and halved lengthways

3 fresh figs, sliced

225 g/8 oz canned asparagus spears, drained

115 g/4 oz smoked salmon, thinly sliced

salt and pepper

115 g/4 oz black olives

extra virgin olive oil, for drizzling

lemon wedges, to garnish

variation

If you like, use the same amount of fresh asparagus spears, instead of canned. Steam or cook in boiling water for 5–7 minutes, or until tender.

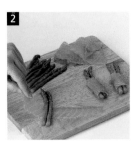

cook's tip

Prosciutto is an Italian, salt-cured ham. The best-known variety is Parma ham from Parma, but other regions in Italy produce their own, such as San Daniele from Friuli.

1 Arrange the tuna, sardines, anchovies, prawns, prosciutto, mozzarella cheese, artichoke hearts and figs on a large serving platter.

2 Wrap 2–3 asparagus spears in each slice of smoked salmon and add to the platter. Season the antipasto to taste with salt and pepper.

3 Sprinkle the olives over the platter and drizzle with the olive oil. Garnish with lemon wedges, then serve immediately or cover with clingfilm and leave to chill in the refrigerator until required, but bring to room temperature before serving.

hummus

serves 4　　　　　**prep: 5 mins** ⏲　　　　　**cook: 0 mins** ⏲

This mildly spicy Middle Eastern dip is easy to make and tastes much better than shop-bought brands. Serve with crudités, such as cauliflower florets, carrot, celery, red pepper batons and breadsticks.

INGREDIENTS

425 g/15 oz canned chickpeas,
drained and rinsed
125 ml/4 fl oz tahini
3 garlic cloves
125 ml/4 fl oz lemon juice
3–4 tbsp water
salt and pepper

TO GARNISH
1 tbsp olive oil
pinch of cayenne pepper
1 tbsp chopped fresh parsley
6 black olives

NUTRITIONAL INFORMATION

Calories	.340
Protein	.13g
Carbohydrate	.17g
Sugars	.1g
Fat	.25g
Saturates	.3g

cook's tip

Tahini is a thick, oily paste made from crushed toasted sesame seeds. It is available from most large supermarkets and health food shops.

1 Mix the chickpeas, tahini, garlic and lemon juice together in a bowl and beat in enough water to make a smooth paste. Season to taste with salt and pepper. Alternatively, place the chickpeas, tahini, garlic, lemon juice and 3 tablespoons of the water in a food processor, season to taste with salt and pepper and process until a smooth paste forms. If the mixture is too thick, add a little more water.

2 Transfer the hummus to a serving dish and make a shallow dip in the centre with the back of a spoon. Pour the olive oil into the dip and sprinkle with cayenne pepper. Garnish with the chopped parsley and olives.

Serve immediately or cover with clingfilm and store in the refrigerator until required.

guacamole

⏱ **cook: 0 mins**   ◔ **prep: 5 mins**   **serves 4**

*Serve this ever-popular Mexican avocado dip with crudités,
crusty bread or spicy tortilla chips. A spoonful placed on plain
grilled steak also makes a wonderful garnish.*

NUTRITIONAL INFORMATION	
Calories	245
Protein	. . . . .3g
Carbohydrate	. . . . .3g
Sugars	. . . . .1g
Fat	. . . . .25g
Saturates	. . . . .6g

INGREDIENTS

3 avocados

2 tbsp lime juice

1 tbsp soured cream

1 tbsp olive oil

½ tsp cayenne pepper

3 spring onions, finely chopped

2 garlic cloves, finely chopped

salt

crusty bread, to serve

variation

Add 2 chopped fresh
tomatoes to the mixture
in Step 2 and replace the
soured cream with natural
yogurt, if you like.

1 Halve and stone the
avocados and, using
a spoon, scoop the flesh into
a bowl. Add the lime juice and
mash roughly with a fork.

2 Add the soured cream,
olive oil, cayenne
pepper, spring onions and
garlic and season to taste with
salt. Mash until thoroughly
blended, but do not make the
guacamole completely smooth.

3 Scoop the mixture into
a serving bowl and
serve immediately with crusty
bread. Alternatively, cover
tightly with clingfilm and
store in the refrigerator for
up to 2 hours.

vegetarian fajitas

cook: 20 mins   **prep: 10 mins**   **serves 6**

NUTRITIONAL INFORMATION	
Calories	.400
Protein	.11g
Carbohydrate	.82g
Sugars	.7g
Fat	.6g
Saturates	.1g

variation

If you don't like dishes too spicy, use 2 fresh chillies instead of 4, or omit them. The fajitas are good served with natural yogurt or soured cream.

These tasty vegetable wraps should be served so hot that your guests can hear them sizzling as you bring them to the table.

INGREDIENTS

2 tbsp corn oil

2 onions, thinly sliced

2 garlic cloves, finely chopped

2 green peppers, deseeded and sliced

2 red peppers, deseeded and sliced

4 fresh green chillies, deseeded and sliced

2 tsp chopped fresh coriander

12 wheat tortillas

225 g/8 oz mushrooms, sliced

salt and pepper

cook's tip

Always wash your hands thoroughly after handling chillies and avoid touching your lips or eyes. If you have sensitive skin, wear rubber gloves.

1 Heat the oil in a heavy-based frying pan. Add the onions and garlic and cook over a low heat, stirring occasionally, for 5 minutes, or until softened. Stir in the green and red peppers, chillies and coriander and cook, stirring occasionally, for 10 minutes.

2 Meanwhile, dry-fry the tortillas, one at a time, for 30 seconds on each side in a separate frying pan. Alternatively, stack the tortillas and heat in a microwave oven according to the packet instructions.

3 Add the mushrooms to the vegetable mixture and cook, stirring constantly, for 1 minute. Season to taste with salt and pepper. Divide the vegetables between the tortillas, roll up and serve immediately.

cured meats with olives & tomatoes

serves 4   **prep: 10 mins** ⏱   **cook: 5 mins** ⏱

This is a typical antipasto dish with cold cured meats, stuffed olives fresh tomatoes, and the extra flavour of basil and balsamic vinegar.

INGREDIENTS

4 plum tomatoes

1 tbsp balsamic vinegar

salt and pepper

6 canned anchovy fillets,
drained and rinsed

2 tbsp capers, drained and rinsed

125 g/4 ½ oz green olives, stoned

175 g/6 oz mixed cured meats, sliced

8 fresh basil leaves

1 tbsp extra virgin olive oil

crusty bread, to serve

NUTRITIONAL INFORMATION

Calories	.312
Protein	.12g
Carbohydrate	.2g
Sugars	.1g
Fat	.28g
Saturates	.1g

---

variation

If you like, you could add slivers of roasted red pepper or artichoke hearts soaked in olive oil to this dish.

cook's tip

The cured meats for this recipe are up to your individual taste. They can include a selection of Parma ham (prosciutto), pancetta, bresaola (dried salt beef) and salame di Milano (pork and beef sausage).

1 Using a sharp knife, cut the tomatoes into evenly sized slices. Sprinkle the tomato slices with the balsamic vinegar and a little salt and pepper to taste, and set aside.

2 Chop the anchovy fillets into pieces measuring about the same length as the olives. Carefully push a piece of anchovy and a caper into the centre of each olive.

3 Arrange the sliced meat on 4 individual serving plates together with the tomatoes, stuffed olives and basil leaves. Lightly drizzle the olive oil over the sliced meat, tomatoes and olives.

4 Serve the antipasto with plenty of fresh crusty bread.

prosciutto & figs

serves 4　　　　**prep: 5 mins** ↻　　　　**cook: 0 mins** ⊙

This classic Italian starter is simplicity itself, but never fails to please. It would be the perfect choice to begin an al fresco meal. Try to find Parma ham or San Daniele as these are the finest prosciuttos.

INGREDIENTS

8 ripe fresh figs

8 thin slices of prosciutto, about 175 g/6 oz

pepper

NUTRITIONAL INFORMATION

Calories 145

Protein 13g

Carbohydrate 10g

Sugars 10g

Fat 6g

Saturates 2g

variation

Arrange 2 slices of prosciutto on each plate and sprinkle with Parmesan cheese shavings. Add 6 olives and drizzle with Vinaigrette (see page 13).

1 Using a sharp knife, cut each fig downwards into quarters from the stalk end, but without cutting all the way through. Gently open out each fruit like a flower and place 2 on each of 4 large serving plates.

2 Arrange 2 slices of prosciutto in decorative folds beside the figs on each plate.

3 Season well with pepper and serve at room temperature, offering the pepper mill at the same time.

mozzarella & tomatoes

⏱ **cook: 0 mins**　　　　　🕐 **prep: 5 mins**　　　　　**serves 4**

Known as insalata tricolore in Italy, this attractive and tasty starter deserves the best ingredients. Try to obtain mozzarella di bufala, *the genuine cheese made from water buffalo milk.*

NUTRITIONAL INFORMATION	
Calories	.446
Protein	.20g
Carbohydrate	.5g
Sugars	.5g
Fat	.39g
Saturates	.13g

INGREDIENTS

600 g/1 lb 5 oz plum tomatoes

300 g/10½ oz mozzarella cheese

16 fresh basil leaves, torn if large

125 ml/4 fl oz extra virgin olive oil, to serve

cook's tip

If you can find them, use fresh plum tomatoes as they are less watery than the standard round varieties. Try to use sun-ripened tomatoes as they have a richer flavour.

1 Using a sharp knife, cut the tomatoes into even slices about 5 mm/¼ inch thick. Drain the mozzarella cheese and discard the whey. Slice the mozzarella cheese evenly.

2 Arrange the tomato and mozzarella slices, over-lapping slightly, in concentric circles on a large serving plate.

3 Sprinkle the basil over the salad and serve immediately with the olive oil for drizzling.

sesame ginger chicken

serves 4

prep: 15 mins, plus 2 hrs marinating

cook: 10 mins

Chunks of chicken breast are marinated in a mixture of lime juice, garlic, sesame oil and fresh ginger to give them a great flavour.

INGREDIENTS

500 g/1 lb 2 oz boneless
chicken breasts

sprigs of fresh mint, to garnish

MARINADE

1 garlic clove, crushed

1 shallot, very finely chopped

2 tbsp sesame oil

1 tbsp nam pla (Thai fish sauce) or
light soy sauce

finely grated rind of 1 lime or ½ lemon
and 2 tbsp lime or lemon juice

1 tsp sesame seeds

2 tsp finely grated fresh root ginger

2 tsp chopped fresh mint

salt and pepper

NUTRITIONAL INFORMATION	
Calories	204
Protein	28g
Carbohydrate	1g
Sugars	0g
Fat	10g
Saturates	2g

variation

If you prefer, substitute fresh coriander for the fresh mint in this recipe, for a slightly mellower taste.

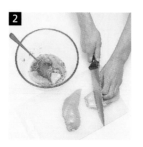

cook's tip

The kebabs taste delicious if dipped into an accompanying bowl of hot chilli sauce. Many major supermarkets stock a variety of suitable ready-made dipping sauces.

1 Place 4 long skewers in cold water to soak. To make the marinade, put the garlic, shallot, sesame oil, nam pla, lime rind and juice, sesame seeds, ginger root and chopped mint into a large, non-metallic bowl. Season with a little salt and pepper and mix together thoroughly.

2 Remove the skin from the chicken breasts and cut the flesh into chunks. Add the chicken to the marinade, stirring to coat completely in the mixture. Cover with clingfilm and chill in the refrigerator for at least 2 hours, so that the flavours are absorbed.

3 Preheat the grill to medium. Thread the chicken on to the pre-soaked skewers. Place them on the rack of a grill pan and baste with the marinade.

4 Place the kebabs under the preheated grill for 8–10 minutes, turning

frequently and basting with the remaining marinade, until the meat is cooked through.

5 Serve the chicken skewers garnished with sprigs of fresh mint.

salads & snacks

The busier the lifestyle, the more important it is to eat a healthy and balanced diet, yet all too often we dash home, grab a bag of crisps, a canned fizzy drink and a chocolate bar before flying out the door again or collapsing in an exhausted heap in front of the television. With only marginally more effort and time, you can prepare tasty and nourishing snacks for just those occasions when you don't feel like eating a whole meal, but you know that your body is craving some nourishment. Salads are the perfect choice when cooking is too much trouble or the weather is hot. Why settle for a limp lettuce leaf and a piece of dried-up cheese, when, in next to no time, you can rustle up Greek Salad (see page 87) with feta, tomatoes and olives, or Caesar Salad (see page 85) with anchovies, croûtons and a unique egg dressing?

A hot snack is just as easy. If you suddenly find yourself entertaining unexpected guests, try Storecupboard Tuna (see page 111); if you need a speedy weekend lunch before the family disperses for the afternoon's activities, serve Spaghetti alla Carbonara (see page 100); if it's too late for breakfast and too early for lunch, Eggs Benedict (see page 114) is the answer; or if you need to fire up some energy before tackling the Christmas shopping, tuck into a steaming plate of Caribbean Cook-up Rice (see page 103).

salade niçoise

cook: 13–17 mins **prep: 12–15 mins** **serves 4**

NUTRITIONAL INFORMATION

Calories 430

Protein 21g

Carbohydrate 15g

Sugars 6g

Fat 32g

Saturates 5g

variation

Use fresh tuna instead of canned. Oil both sides of 2 tuna steaks and cook in a griddle pan for 1–2 minutes. Slice and add to the salad in Step 3.

This Provençal dish is probably the best-known and best-loved classic salad in the Western world. The combination of beans, tuna, tomatoes and olives is virtually irresistible.

INGREDIENTS

2 eggs

12 small salad potatoes, such as Pink Fir Apple or Maris Bard

salt

115 g/4 oz green beans

2 cos lettuces or 3 Little Gem lettuces

200 g/7 oz canned tuna in oil

6 canned anchovy fillets

4 tomatoes

4 spring onions

12 black olives

2 tbsp bottled capers, drained

2 tbsp pine kernels

DRESSING

6 tbsp extra virgin olive oil

2 tbsp tarragon vinegar

1 tsp Dijon mustard

1 garlic clove, finely chopped

cook's tip

There are lots of different herb vinegars available in most large supermarkets, but if you cannot find tarragon vinegar, then use the same amount of white wine vinegar instead.

1 Cook the eggs, potatoes and beans simultaneously. Place the eggs in a saucepan and cover with cold water. Bring to the boil, then reduce the heat and boil gently for 12 minutes. Cook the potatoes in a saucepan of lightly salted boiling water for 12–15 minutes, or until tender, and cook the green beans in a separate saucepan of lightly salted boiling water for 3–5 minutes.

2 Meanwhile, prepare all the remaining ingredients. Roughly chop the lettuces, drain and flake the tuna, then drain the anchovies and halve them lengthways. Chop the tomatoes and slice the spring onions. To make the dressing, place all the ingredients in a large salad bowl and beat well to mix.

3 Drain the beans and refresh in cold water. Add to the salad bowl with the lettuces, tuna, anchovies, tomatoes, spring onions, olives and capers. Drain the eggs, cool under cold running water and reserve. Drain the potatoes and add to the salad. Lightly toast the pine kernels in a dry frying pan, shaking the frying pan frequently, for 1–2 minutes, or until golden. Sprinkle them over the salad. Shell and chop the eggs and add them to the salad.

4 Whisk the dressing again, add it to the salad, toss to coat and serve.

mexican tomato salad

serves 4　　　　**prep: 5 mins** ⏱　　　　**cook: 0 mins** ⏱

This easy and economical salad would make an ideal light vegetarian lunch, served with some fresh crusty bread, or it would make an excellent accompaniment to a barbecue.

INGREDIENTS

600 g/1 lb 5 oz tomatoes, peeled, deseeded and roughly chopped

1 onion, thinly sliced and pushed out into rings

400 g/14 oz canned kidney beans, drained and rinsed

1 fresh green chilli, deseeded and thinly sliced

3 tbsp chopped fresh coriander

3 tbsp olive oil

1 garlic clove, finely chopped

4 tbsp lime juice

salt and pepper

NUTRITIONAL INFORMATION

Calories 210

Protein 8g

Carbohydrate 25g

Sugars 10g

Fat 9g

Saturates 1g

---

variation

You could substitute two canned chipotle chillies, drained and rinsed, for the fresh chilli, and broad beans for the kidney beans, if you prefer.

1 Place the chopped tomatoes and onion slices into a large serving bowl and mix well. Stir in the kidney beans.

2 Mix the chilli, coriander, olive oil, garlic and lime juice together in a jug and season to taste with salt and pepper.

3 Pour the dressing over the salad and toss thoroughly. Serve immediately or cover with clingfilm and leave to chill in the refrigerator until required.

cook's tip

If this salad has been made in advance and stored in the refrigerator, then bring it back to room temperature before serving.

caesar salad

cook: 6 mins **prep: 5–10 mins** **serves 4**

NUTRITIONAL INFORMATION

Calories 506

Protein 16g

Carbohydrate 26g

Sugars 2g

Fat 38g

Saturates 9g

variation

Replace the cos and Little Gem lettuces with mixed salad leaves, such as lollo rosso, oakleaf and rocket.

Created by Caesar Cardini in the 1920s, the classic version of this salad includes raw egg in the dressing, but in this recipe, the egg is very lightly cooked first.

INGREDIENTS

6 tbsp olive oil

1 large egg

2 cos lettuces or 3 Little Gem lettuces

2 tbsp lemon juice

salt and pepper

8 canned anchovy fillets, drained and roughly chopped

85 g/3 oz fresh Parmesan cheese shavings

GARLIC CROUTONS

4 tbsp olive oil

2 garlic cloves

5 slices white bread, crusts removed, cut into 1-cm/½-inch cubes

cook's tip

Don't leave the salad standing around too long after the dressing has been added or the lettuce will go soggy and the salad will be unusable.

1 Bring a small, heavy-based saucepan of water to the boil.

2 Meanwhile, make the garlic croûtons. Heat the olive oil in a heavy-based frying pan. Add the garlic and diced bread and cook, stirring and tossing frequently, for 4–5 minutes, or until the bread is crispy and golden all over.

Remove from the frying pan with a slotted spoon and drain on kitchen paper.

3 While the bread is frying, add the egg to the boiling water and cook for 1 minute, then remove from the saucepan and reserve.

4 Arrange the lettuce leaves in a salad bowl.

Mix the remaining olive oil and lemon juice together, then season to taste with salt and pepper. Crack the egg into the dressing and whisk to blend. Pour the dressing over the lettuce leaves, toss well, then add the croûtons and anchovies and toss the salad again. Sprinkle with Parmesan cheese shavings and serve.

chef's salad

serves 6 **prep: 5 mins** **cook: 0 mins**

The name of the chef who was responsible for this substantial salad with its piquant Thousand Island Dressing seems to be lost in the mists of time – but he was clearly a good chap.

INGREDIENTS

1 iceberg lettuce, shredded
175 g/6 oz cooked ham,
cut into thin strips
175 g/6 oz cooked tongue,
cut into thin strips
350 g/12 oz cooked chicken,
cut into thin strips
175 g/6 oz Gruyère cheese
4 tomatoes, quartered
3 hard-boiled eggs, shelled
and quartered
400 ml/14 fl oz Thousand Island
Dressing (see page 13)

NUTRITIONAL INFORMATION

Calories	.730
Protein	.41g
Carbohydrate	.5g
Sugars	.5g
Fat	.61g
Saturates	.15g

cook's tip

This is a good salad to take on a picnic. Pack the salad in a large rigid container and pack the dressing in a separate covered bowl, then serve the salad and dressing separately.

1 Arrange the lettuce on a large serving platter. Arrange the cold meat decoratively on top.

2 Cut the Gruyère cheese into batons.

3 Arrange the cheese batons over the salad, and the tomato and egg quarters around the edge of the platter. Serve the salad immediately, handing round the dressing separately.

greek salad

cook: 0 mins **prep: 10 mins** **serves 4**

As you might expect, this is the perfect salad for a very hot day, as the piquancy of the feta cheese contrasts with the refreshing cucumber, succulent tomatoes and fruity olives.

NUTRITIONAL INFORMATION	
Calories	373
Protein	17g
Carbohydrate	2g
Sugars	2g
Fat	33g
Saturates	2g

INGREDIENTS

1 cucumber, halved lengthways

18 cherry tomatoes, halved

400 g/14 oz feta cheese

4 tbsp extra virgin olive oil

1 tbsp lemon juice

12 black olives

salt and pepper

ciabatta bread, to serve

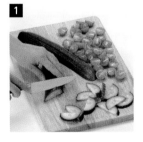

1 Using a sharp knife, cut the cucumber halves into 1-cm/½-inch thick slices and divide between 4 individual serving plates with the cherry tomatoes.

2 Crumble the feta cheese and sprinkle the olives equally over the salads.

3 Drizzle with the olive oil and lemon juice. Season to taste with salt and pepper, but bear in mind that both the olives and the feta will be quite salty. Toss lightly and serve with ciabatta.

cook's tip

Although originally made from ewe's milk, much modern feta is now made from cow's milk. It is worth looking for the genuine cheese, made either in Greece or Bulgaria.

russian salad

serves 4 **prep: 10 mins** **cook: 20 mins**

First created in France for the delectation of aristocrats who had fled the Russian revolution, the recipe for this salad has itself undergone some dramatic changes over the years.

INGREDIENTS

115 g/4 oz salad potatoes, such as Pink Fir Apple or Maris Bard

115 g/4 oz frozen or shelled fresh broad beans

115 g/4 oz baby carrots

115 g/4 oz baby sweetcorn

115 g/4 oz baby turnips

115 g/4 oz button mushrooms, cut into thin batons

350 g/12 oz cooked peeled prawns, deveined

125 ml/4 fl oz mayonnaise

1 tbsp lemon juice

2 tbsp bottled capers, drained and rinsed

salt and pepper

2 tbsp extra virgin olive oil

2 hard-boiled eggs, shelled and halved

4 canned anchovy fillets, drained and halved

paprika, to garnish

NUTRITIONAL INFORMATION

Calories	.512
Protein	.32g
Carbohydrate	.13g
Sugars	.5g
Fat	.37g
Saturates	.6g

variation

Replace the button mushrooms with the same amount of chestnut mushrooms, if you prefer.

cook's tip

If you find canned anchovies too salty, then place them in a small bowl and cover with milk. Leave to soak for 10 minutes, then drain and pat dry with kitchen paper.

1 Cook the potatoes, broad beans, carrots, sweetcorn and turnips simultaneously. Cook the potatoes in a large saucepan of lightly salted boiling water for 20 minutes. Cook the broad beans in a small saucepan of lightly salted water for 3 minutes, then drain, refresh under cold running water and reserve.

Cook the carrots, sweetcorn and turnips in a large saucepan of lightly salted boiling water for 6 minutes.

2 Mix the mushrooms and prawns together in a bowl. Mix the mayonnaise and lemon juice together in a separate bowl, then fold half the mixture into the prawn mixture. Fold in the capers and season to taste with salt and pepper.

3 Drain the mixed vegetables, refresh under cold running water and tip into a bowl. When the potatoes are cooked, drain, refresh under cold running water and tip into the bowl. Pop the broad beans out of their skins by pinching them between your finger and thumb and add to the bowl. Add the olive oil and toss to coat. Divide the potatoes and vegetables between serving plates and top with the prawn mixture. Place a hard-boiled egg half in the centre of each and decorate with the halved anchovies. Dust the eggs with paprika and serve with the remaining mayonnaise mixture.

lentil pâté

serves 4 **prep: 30 mins, plus 1 hr chilling** **cook: 1 hr 15 mins**

Red lentils are used in this spicy recipe for speed because they do not require any pre-soaking. The pâté makes a tasty and unusual starter for a vegetarian dinner party.

INGREDIENTS

1 tbsp vegetable oil, plus extra for greasing

1 onion, chopped

2 garlic cloves, crushed

1 tsp garam masala

½ tsp ground coriander

850 ml/1½ pints Vegetable Stock (see page 13)

175 g/6 oz red lentils

1 small egg

2 tbsp milk

2 tbsp mango chutney

2 tbsp chopped fresh parsley

fresh parsley sprigs, to garnish

TO SERVE

salad leaves

toast

NUTRITIONAL INFORMATION	
Calories	.267
Protein	.14g
Carbohydrate	.37g
Sugars	.12g
Fat	.8g
Saturates	.1g

variation

You can use other types of lentils, such as Puy lentils, for this recipe, but you will need to include soaking time in your preparations.

cook's tip

It is always better to make your own stock, if you can find the time, rather than use stock cubes, because the flavour of homemade stock is far superior.

1 Heat the oil in a large saucepan and sauté the onion and garlic, stirring constantly, for 2–3 minutes. Add the spices and cook for a further 30 seconds. Stir in the Stock and lentils and bring the mixture to the boil. Reduce the heat and simmer for 20 minutes, until the lentils are cooked and softened. Remove the saucepan from the heat and drain off any excess moisture.

2 Put the mixture in a food processor and add the egg, milk, mango chutney and parsley. Process until smooth.

3 Grease and line the base of a 450-g/1-lb loaf tin and spoon in the mixture, levelling the surface. Cover and cook in a preheated oven, 200°C/400°F/Gas Mark 6, for 40–45 minutes, or until firm to the touch.

4 Cool in the tin for 20 minutes, then chill in the refrigerator for 1 hour.

5 Turn out the pâté on to a serving plate, slice and garnish with fresh parsley. Serve with salad leaves and lightly cooked toast.

smoked fish & potato pâté

serves 4 **prep: 20 mins** ⏱ **cook: 10 mins** ♨

This smoked fish pâté is given a tart, fruity flavour by fresh gooseberries, which complement the fish perfectly.

INGREDIENTS

650 g/1 lb 7 oz floury potatoes, diced	1 tbsp capers
300 g/10½ oz smoked mackerel, skinned and flaked	1 gherkin, chopped
	1 tbsp chopped dill pickle
75 g/2¾ oz cooked gooseberries	1 tbsp chopped fresh dill
2 tsp lemon juice	salt and pepper
2 tbsp low-fat crème fraîche	lemon wedges, to garnish
	toast or warm crusty bread, to serve

NUTRITIONAL INFORMATION

Calories	.418
Protein	.18g
Carbohydrate	.32g
Sugars	.4g
Fat	.25g
Saturates	.6g

variation

Add a slightly different flavour to the pâté by using chopped fresh parsley or snipped chives instead of the fresh dill.

cook's tip

Use stewed, canned or bottled cooked gooseberries for convenience and to save time, or when fresh gooseberries are out of season.

1 Cook the potatoes in a saucepan of boiling water for 10 minutes, or until tender, then drain well.

2 Place the cooked potatoes in a food processor or blender, add the smoked mackerel and process for 30 seconds, or until fairly smooth. Alternatively, place the ingredients in a bowl and mash with a fork.

3 Add the cooked gooseberries, lemon juice and crème fraîche to the fish and potato mixture. Blend for a further 10 seconds, or mash well.

4 Stir in the capers, gherkin, dill pickle and dill. Season well with salt and pepper.

5 Turn the fish pâté into a serving dish, garnish with lemon wedges and serve with slices of toast or chunks of warm crusty bread.

shallots à la grecque

serves 4 **prep: 10 mins** ⏲ **cook: 15 mins** ⏲

This is a well-known method of cooking vegetables using olive oil, honey and wine, and tastes perfect served with a crisp salad.

INGREDIENTS

450 g/1 lb shallots

3 tbsp olive oil

3 tbsp clear honey

2 tbsp garlic wine vinegar

3 tbsp dry white wine

1 tbsp tomato purée

2 celery sticks, sliced

2 tomatoes, deseeded and chopped

salt and pepper

chopped celery leaves, to garnish

NUTRITIONAL INFORMATION

Calories 200

Protein 2g

Carbohydrate 28g

Sugars 26g

Fat 9g

Saturates 1g

variation

You can substitute the shallots with small onions or onion wedges, which taste just as good cooked à la Grecque.

1 Peel the shallots. Heat the oil in a large saucepan, add the shallots and cook, stirring, for 3–5 minutes, or until they begin to brown.

2 Add the honey and cook over a high heat for a further 30 seconds, then add the garlic wine vinegar and white wine, stirring well.

3 Stir in the tomato purée, celery and tomatoes and bring the mixture to the boil. Cook over a high heat for 5–6 minutes. Season to taste and leave to cool slightly.

4 Garnish with chopped celery leaves and serve warm. Alternatively, chill in the refrigerator before serving.

baked fennel

cook: 35 mins   **prep: 10 mins**   **serves 4**

Fennel is used extensively in northern Italy. It is a very versatile vegetable, which is good cooked or used raw in salads.

NUTRITIONAL INFORMATION

Calories	111
Protein	7g
Carbohydrate	7g
Sugars	6g
Fat	7g
Saturates	3g

INGREDIENTS

2 fennel bulbs

2 celery sticks, cut into 7.5-cm/
3-inch lengths

6 sun-dried tomatoes, halved

200 g/7 oz passata

2 tsp dried oregano

50 g/1¾ oz Parmesan cheese,
freshly grated, plus extra to garnish

crusty bread, to serve (optional)

variation

Sprinkle pine kernels over the dish before serving to add a little protein and extra flavour.

1 Preheat the oven to 190°C/375°F/Gas Mark 5. Using a sharp knife, trim the fennel, discarding any tough outer leaves, and cut the bulb into quarters.

2 Bring a large pan of water to the boil, add the fennel and celery and cook for 8–10 minutes, or until just tender. Remove with a slotted spoon and drain.

3 Place the fennel pieces, celery and sun-dried tomatoes in a large, ovenproof dish. Mix the passata with the oregano and pour the mixture over the fennel.

4 Sprinkle with the Parmesan cheese and bake in the preheated oven for 20 minutes, or until piping hot. Serve as a starter with crusty bread, or as a vegetable side dish, garnished with Parmesan cheese shavings.

chicken goujons

cook: 15 mins   **prep: 15 mins**   **serves 4**

NUTRITIONAL INFORMATION

Calories	.655
Protein	.36g
Carbohydrate	.48g
Sugars	.3g
Fat	.37g
Saturates	.16g

Popular with adults and children alike, these tasty strips of chicken would make a good lunch served with salad and new potatoes or, equally, could be served on their own as a starter for six.

INGREDIENTS

4 skinless, boneless chicken breasts, about 115 g/4 oz each

3 tbsp plain flour

sunflower oil, for deep-frying

175 g/6 oz dried breadcrumbs

1 tsp ground coriander

2 tsp paprika

salt and pepper

2 eggs, lightly beaten

CHEESE & CHIVE DIP

115 g/4 oz cream cheese

150 ml/5 fl oz soured cream

3 tbsp snipped fresh chives

salt and pepper

paprika, for sprinkling

TO GARNISH

lemon wedges

fresh chives

variation

Instead of the cheese & chive dip, serve the goujons with Guacamole (see page 69), Thousand Island Dressing (see page 13) or just mayonnaise.

cook's tip

When deep-frying, make sure that the oil is at the correct temperature before cooking. If it is too hot it will burn the food on the outside, but leave the inside raw.

1 Place the chicken breasts between 2 sheets of clingfilm and beat with the flat side of a meat mallet or with the side of a rolling pin until about 5 mm/ ¼ inch thick. Slice diagonally into 2.5-cm/1-inch strips. Place the flour in a polythene bag and add the chicken strips, a few at a time, shaking well until the chicken is coated.

2 Heat the sunflower oil in a large, heavy-based saucepan to 180–190°C/ 350–375°F, or until a cube of bread browns in 30 seconds. Meanwhile, mix the breadcrumbs, coriander and paprika together, season to taste with salt and pepper and spread out on a plate. Dip the chicken strips first in the beaten egg and then in the

breadcrumb mixture. When the oil is hot, deep-fry the goujons, in batches, until crisp and golden all over. Remove from the saucepan with a slotted spoon and drain on kitchen paper.

3 Meanwhile, make the dip. Mix the cream cheese, soured cream and chives together in a serving

bowl, season to taste with salt and pepper and sprinkle with paprika. Transfer the goujons to a large serving plate and, garnish with lemon wedges. Garnish the dip with chives and serve with the goujons.

deep-fried seafood

serves 4   **prep: 5 mins**   **cook: 15 mins**

*Deep-fried seafood is a popular dish all around the Mediterranean,
where fish of every shape and flavour is fresh and abundant.*

INGREDIENTS

200 g/7 oz prepared squid

200 g/7 oz tiger prawns,
peeled and deveined

150 g/5½ oz whitebait

oil, for deep-frying

50 g/1 ½ oz plain flour

1 tsp dried basil

salt and pepper

TO SERVE

garlic mayonnaise

lemon wedges

NUTRITIONAL INFORMATION	
Calories	.393
Protein	.27g
Carbohydrate	.12g
Sugars	.0.2g
Fat	.26g
Saturates	.3g

variation

To give this dish more of
an Eastern flavour, try
serving the deep-fried
seafood with chilli sauce
and lime wedges.

1 Rinse the squid, prawns
and whitebait under
cold running water to remove
any dirt or grit. Using a sharp
knife, slice the squid into rings,
leaving the tentacles whole.

2 Heat the oil in a
large saucepan to
180–190°C/350–375°F, or
until a cube of bread browns
in 30 seconds.

3 Place the flour in a
bowl, add the basil
and season with salt and
pepper to taste. Mix well.
Roll the squid, prawns and
whitebait in the seasoned flour
until coated. Shake off any
excess flour.

4 Cook the seafood in
the hot oil, in batches,
for 2–3 minutes, or until crispy
and golden all over. Remove all
of the seafood with a slotted
spoon and leave to drain
thoroughly on kitchen paper.

5 Transfer the seafood to
serving plates and serve
with garlic mayonnaise and a
few lemon wedges.

aubergine dipping platter

⏱ **cook: 10 mins**   ◔ **prep: 15 mins**   **serves 4**

Dipping platters are healthy and delicious – great for informal occasions, or for serving with drinks before dinner.

NUTRITIONAL INFORMATION

Calories	.81
Protein	.4g
Carbohydrate	.5g
Sugars	.4g
Fat	.5g
Saturates	.1g

INGREDIENTS

1 aubergine

3 tbsp sesame seeds

1 tsp sesame oil

grated rind and juice of ½ lime

1 small shallot, diced

salt and pepper

1 tsp sugar

1 red chilli, deseeded and sliced

125 g/4½ oz broccoli florets

2 carrots, cut into matchsticks

8 baby corn cobs, halved lengthways

2 celery sticks, cut into matchsticks

1 baby red cabbage, cut into 8 wedges

variation

You can vary the selection of vegetables, depending on your preference. Other vegetables you could use include cauliflower florets and cucumber sticks.

1 Peel the aubergine and cut the flesh into 2.5-cm/1-inch cubes. Cook in a saucepan of boiling water for 7–8 minutes.

2 Meanwhile, place the sesame seeds in a dry pan over a low heat and roast for 1–2 minutes, until golden. Place the sesame seeds in a food processor with the oil and blend, or crush them with the oil using a pestle and mortar.

3 Add the aubergine, lime rind and juice, shallot, ½ tsp salt, pepper, sugar and chilli in that order to the sesame seeds. Process, or chop and mash by hand, until smooth. Adjust the seasoning to taste, then spoon the dip into a bowl.

4 Serve the dipping platter surrounded by the broccoli, carrots, baby corn, celery and red cabbage.

spaghetti alla carbonara

serves 4   **prep: 10 mins**   **cook: 10 mins**

This traditional Italian recipe is one of the quickest, simplest, most economical and tastiest of pasta dishes. It is not difficult to cook, but it is important to keep everything really hot so that the egg cooks lightly when it is added at the end, but doesn't scramble.

INGREDIENTS

450 g/1 lb dried spaghetti

175 g/6 oz rindless streaky bacon, diced

1 garlic clove, finely chopped

3 eggs, lightly beaten

salt and pepper

4 tbsp fresh Parmesan cheese shavings

NUTRITIONAL INFORMATION

Calories 607

Protein 29g

Carbohydrate 84g

Sugars 4g

Fat 29g

Saturates 20g

variation

For additional flavour, you could add 115 g/4 oz sliced button or chestnut mushrooms to the frying pan in Step 2.

1 Bring a large, heavy-based saucepan of lightly salted water to the boil. Add the pasta, return to the boil and cook for 8–10 minutes, or until tender but still firm to the bite.

2 Meanwhile, cook the bacon and garlic in a heavy-based, dry frying pan over a medium heat for 5 minutes, or until crisp-tender. Remove from the frying pan and drain on kitchen paper.

3 Drain the pasta and return it to the saucepan, but do not return to the heat. Add the bacon and garlic and the eggs. Season to taste with salt and pepper. Toss thoroughly with 2 large forks. Add half the Parmesan cheese and toss again. Transfer to a warmed serving dish, sprinkle with the remaining Parmesan cheese and serve immediately.

cook's tip

It is best to buy fresh Parmesan cheese, available in most supermarkets in a block, and grate or shave it yourself, as it tastes much better than ready-grated Parmesan cheese.

caribbean cook-up rice

⏲ **cook: 25 mins**   ◔ **prep: 5 mins**   **serves 4**

NUTRITIONAL INFORMATION

Calories 674

Protein 16g

Carbohydrate 118g

Sugars 5g

Fat 19g

Saturates 12g

Gunga peas, also known as gungo, pigeon and Jamaica peas, are popular in Africa, India and, most of all, in the Caribbean. They have a nutty flavour, more like a bean than a pea.

INGREDIENTS

25 g/1 oz butter	600 ml/1 pint Vegetable Stock
1 onion, chopped	(see page 13)
1 garlic clove, finely chopped	55 g/2 oz creamed coconut
1 carrot, chopped	1 fresh green chilli, deseeded
400 g/14 oz canned gunga peas,	and chopped
drained and rinsed	salt and pepper
1 cinnamon stick	450 g/1 lb long-grain rice
1 fresh thyme sprig	

variation

While not authentic, you could substitute canned chickpeas if gunga peas are not available.

cook's tip

When cooking with rice, especially long-grain and basmati, always rinse it under cold running water first as this removes all the excess starch.

1 Melt the butter in a large, heavy-based frying pan or flameproof casserole. Add the onion and garlic and cook over a low heat, stirring occasionally, for 5 minutes, or until softened.

2 Add the carrot, gunga peas, cinnamon stick, thyme, Vegetable Stock, coconut and chilli, stir well and season to taste with salt and pepper. Bring to the boil, stirring frequently.

3 Add the rice and return to the boil, then reduce the heat, cover and simmer for 15 minutes, or until the rice is tender and all the liquid has been absorbed. Remove and discard the thyme sprig and cinnamon stick, then fluff up the rice with a fork. Transfer to individual serving dishes and serve immediately.

speedy vegetable pilau

serves 4   **prep: 5 mins** ⏲   **cook: 15–20 mins** ♨

You can serve this quick, tasty rice dish as a filling, vegetarian snack or as an accompaniment to meat or fish, in which case, this quantity would serve about six people.

INGREDIENTS

450 g/1 lb basmati rice

2 tbsp sunflower oil

2 garlic cloves, finely chopped

½ cinnamon stick

2 cardamom pods

½ tsp black cumin seeds

1 tomato, sliced

55 g/2 oz baby button mushrooms

85 g/3 oz shelled peas

700 ml/1¼ pints Vegetable Stock
(see page 13)

NUTRITIONAL INFORMATION

Calories	.474
Protein	.10g
Carbohydrate	.93g
Sugars	.1g
Fat	.6g
Saturates	.1g

variation

Use the same amount of sliced chestnut mushrooms instead of the button ones, and if shelled peas are not available, then use frozen instead.

cook's tip

If you have time, soak the rice in a large bowl of cold water for 10 minutes before cooking, as this helps to lighten the grain.

1 Rinse the basmati rice thoroughly in 2–3 changes of water, drain well and reserve until required.

2 Heat the sunflower oil in a large, heavy-based saucepan or flameproof casserole. Add the garlic, cinnamon stick, cardamom and cumin and cook, stirring constantly, for 1 minute. Add the tomato and mushrooms and cook, stirring constantly, for 3 minutes.

3 Stir in the rice and peas and cook for 1 minute, stirring to coat the grains, then add the Vegetable Stock and bring to the boil. Reduce the heat, cover and simmer for 10–15 minutes, or until the rice is tender and the liquid has been absorbed. Remove and discard the cinnamon stick and serve immediately.

singapore noodles

cook: 5 mins

prep: 5 mins, plus 10 mins soaking

serves 4

NUTRITIONAL INFORMATION

Calories 430

Protein 27g

Carbohydrate 38g

Sugars 1g

Fat 18g

Saturates 4g

variation

Replace the pork and chicken batons with the same amount of cooked minced pork and chicken and use a red pepper instead of a green pepper.

This spicy noodle dish is easily adapted to include whatever you have to hand – you could substitute Thai fish cakes for the prawns, for example. Reduce the amount of preparation time by cutting up the meat and vegetables while the noodles are soaking.

INGREDIENTS

175 g/6 oz rice noodles	85 g/3 oz cooked chicken,
5 tbsp groundnut oil	cut into batons
salt	1 green pepper, deseeded and
2 spring onions, sliced	cut into batons
85 g/3 oz cooked peeled prawns	½ tsp sugar
175 g/6 oz cooked pork,	2 tsp curry powder
cut into batons	2 tsp dark soy sauce

cook's tip

Dark soy sauce is darker, sweeter and stronger than light soy sauce. It goes well with meat dishes containing beef, pork or duck.

1 Place the noodles in a large bowl and pour over enough warm water to cover. Leave to soak for 10 minutes, or according to the packet instructions. Drain well and pat dry with kitchen paper. Heat half the groundnut oil in a preheated wok or large, heavy-based frying pan. Add the soaked noodles and a pinch of salt and stir-fry for

2 minutes. Transfer to a heatproof bowl with a slotted spoon and keep warm.

2 Add the remaining groundnut oil to the wok or frying pan. When it is hot, add the spring onions, prawns, pork, chicken, green pepper, sugar, curry powder and a pinch of salt and stir-fry for 1 minute.

3 Return the noodles to the wok or frying pan and stir-fry, tossing the ingredients together, for a further 2 minutes. Stir in the soy sauce and serve.

cheese fritters

serves 4　　　　**prep: 10 mins** ⏲　　　　**cook: 15 mins** ⏲

These crisp little savoury snacks can be served at any time of the day, and make lovely hot nibbles for a party or buffet table.

INGREDIENTS

225 g/8 oz cream cheese

55 g/2 oz plain flour

2 large potatoes, grated

1 egg, lightly beaten

75–125 ml/2½–4 fl oz milk

salt and pepper

sunflower oil, for frying

NUTRITIONAL INFORMATION

Calories	.467
Protein	.7g
Carbohydrate	.27g
Sugars	.2g
Fat	.38g
Saturates	.19g

cook's tip

You can also cook these tasty cheese fritters in a deep-fryer for 2–4 minutes and serve with a hot chilli sauce or plain mayonnaise for dipping.

1 Beat the cream cheese in a bowl until it is smooth and soft. Sift the flour into a separate bowl and fold in the cream cheese. Beat in the grated potatoes, egg and enough milk to make a smooth, thick batter. Season to taste with salt and pepper.

2 Pour the sunflower oil into a heavy-based frying pan to a depth of 2.5 cm/1 inch and heat. Add spoonfuls of the batter to the frying pan, spacing them well apart, and cook for 2–3 minutes on each side, or until golden brown.

3 Remove the fritters from the frying pan with a fish slice and drain on kitchen paper. Keep warm while you cook the remainder, then serve immediately.

cheese aigrettes

 cook: 20 mins   prep: 10 mins   serves 6

Light-as-air choux puffs are deep-fried to make these sensational cheese snacks, which are perfect served as party food.

NUTRITIONAL INFORMATION	
Calories	.354
Protein	.12g
Carbohydrate	.13g
Sugars	.0g
Fat	.28g
Saturates	.14g

INGREDIENTS

100 g/3½ oz plain flour

½ tsp paprika

salt and pepper

6 tbsp butter, diced

200 ml/7 fl oz water

3 eggs, lightly beaten

85 g/3 oz Gruyère cheese, grated

sunflower oil, for deep-frying

55 g/2 oz freshly grated
Parmesan cheese

cook's tip

When deep-frying, either use a deep-fryer or a large, deep, heavy-based saucepan. Do not fill the deep-fryer more than half full with oil and the saucepan more than a third full.

1 Sift the flour, paprika and ½ teaspoon salt together on to a sheet of greaseproof paper or baking paper. Place the butter in a large, heavy-based saucepan, pour in the water and heat gently. The moment the butter has melted and the liquid begins to boil, tip in the flour mixture and beat

vigorously with a wooden spoon until the dough comes away from the side of the saucepan.

2 Remove the saucepan from the heat and leave to cool for 5 minutes. Gradually beat in the eggs to give a stiff, dropping consistency – you may not

need all of them. Stir in the Gruyère cheese.

3 Heat the sunflower oil to 180–190°C/ 350–375°F, or until a cube of bread browns in 30 seconds. Shape balls of choux dough between 2 teaspoons and drop them into the oil. Cook for 3–4 minutes, or until golden

brown. Remove with a slotted spoon, drain on kitchen paper and keep warm until all the aigrettes are cooked. Pile on to a warmed serving dish, sprinkle with grated Parmesan cheese and serve immediately.

storecupboard tuna

cook: 25 mins   prep: 5 mins   serves 4

NUTRITIONAL INFORMATION

Calories	.458
Protein	.23g
Carbohydrate	.38g
Sugars	.12g
Fat	.25g
Saturates	.11g

All the flavour of a fish pie with none of the hard work, this dish is perfect for those days when you don't feel much like shopping or cooking. Serve with crusty bread for a more substantial meal.

INGREDIENTS

25 g/1 oz butter, plus
extra for greasing

25 g/1 oz plain flour

300 ml/10 fl oz milk

55 g/2 oz Cheddar cheese, grated

200 g/7 oz canned tuna in oil

325 g/11½ oz canned
sweetcorn, drained

salt and pepper

2 tomatoes, thinly sliced

70 g/2½ oz plain crisps

variation

Substitute canned mackerel for tuna and Red Leicester for the Cheddar. If you prefer flavoured crisps, like cheese and onion, use these instead of plain.

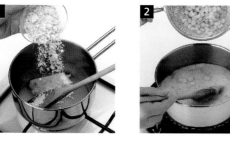  

cook's tip

You can cook this dish in the microwave. Place the mixture in a bowl, cover and cook on Medium for 5 minutes, or until piping hot, stirring halfway through. Transfer to a serving plate, add the crisps and serve.

1 Preheat the oven to 180°C/350°F/Gas Mark 4. Melt the butter in a large, heavy-based saucepan. Sprinkle in the flour and cook, stirring constantly, for 1 minute. Remove the saucepan from the heat and gradually whisk in the milk. Return to the heat, bring to the boil and cook, whisking constantly, for 2 minutes.

2 Remove the saucepan from the heat and stir in the grated cheese. Flake the tuna and add it to the mixture with the oil from the can. Stir in the sweetcorn and season to taste with salt and pepper.

3 Lightly grease a large ovenproof dish. Line the dish with the tomato slices, then spoon in the tuna mixture. Crumble the crisps over the top and bake in the preheated oven for 20 minutes. Serve.

wild mushroom omelettes

serves 2   **prep: 5 mins** 🕒   **cook: 7–8 mins** 🕒

Eggs are a great stand-by when time is short, but they don't have to be boring. An omelette with a creamy mushroom filling, perhaps served with a green salad, is a dish fit for a king.

INGREDIENTS

25 g/1 oz butter

6 eggs, lightly beaten

salt and pepper

WILD MUSHROOM FILLING

25 g/1 oz butter

150 g/5½ oz wild mushrooms, sliced

2 tbsp crème fraîche

NUTRITIONAL INFORMATION

Calories	.457
Protein	.21g
Carbohydrate	.2g
Sugars	.0g
Fat	.41g
Saturates	.21g

cook's tip

Use whatever wild mushrooms are available, such as morels, chanterelles and flat or field mushrooms. To clean, rinse morels and chanterelles in cold water and shake dry. Wipe field mushrooms with a damp cloth.

1 To make the wild mushroom filling, heat the butter in a large, heavy-based frying pan. Add the mushrooms and cook over a low heat, stirring occasionally, for 5 minutes. Stir in the crème fraîche and season to taste with salt and pepper. Keep warm.

2 To make the omelettes, melt half the butter in an omelette pan or small frying pan over a medium–high heat. Season the eggs to taste with salt and pepper, add half to the omelette pan and stir with a fork. As the egg sets, draw it towards the centre and tilt the omelette pan so that the uncooked egg runs underneath. Cook until the underside of the omelette is golden and set, but the top is still moist.

3 Remove the omelette pan from the heat. Spoon half the mushroom mixture along a line just to one side of the centre of the omelette. Flip the other side over and slide the omelette on to a plate. Keep warm. Melt the remaining butter and cook a second omelette in the same way. Serve immediately.

omelettes with fines herbes

⏱ **cook: 4 mins**   ⏱ **prep: 10 mins**   **serves 2**

This subtly flavoured omelette would go well with a tomato salad and Vinaigrette dressing (see page 13) or mixed salad leaves for a light, summery lunch.

NUTRITIONAL INFORMATION	
Calories	.320
Protein	.20g
Carbohydrate	.1g
Sugars	.0g
Fat	.27g
Saturates	.11g

INGREDIENTS

6 eggs

4 tbsp chopped fresh parsley

4 tbsp chopped fresh tarragon

4 tbsp chopped fresh chervil

2 tbsp snipped fresh chives

salt and pepper

25 g/1 oz butter

mixed salad leaves, to serve

cook's tip

French fines herbes is a mix of four fresh aromatic herbs – tarragon, chives, parsley and chervil. However, if you cannot find some of these herbs, then use marjoram, oregano or dill instead.

1 Beat the eggs with the parsley, tarragon, chervil and chives. Season to taste with salt and pepper.

2 Melt half the butter in an omelette pan or small, heavy-based frying pan. Add half the egg mixture and stir with a fork. As the egg sets, draw it towards the centre and tilt the omelette pan so that the uncooked egg runs underneath. Cook until the underside of the omelette is golden and set, but the top is still moist.

3 Remove the omelette pan from the heat and slide the omelette on to a plate, flipping the pan gently so that the omelette folds. Keep warm. Melt the remaining butter and cook a second omelette in the same way. Serve immediately with mixed salad leaves.

eggs benedict

serves 4   **prep: 5 mins** ⏰   **cook: 25 mins** ⏱

This is really just a sophisticated version of the classic combination of ham and eggs and is just as satisfying.

INGREDIENTS

25 g/1 oz butter	HOLLANDAISE SAUCE
4 slices ham	3 egg yolks
2 muffins, split in half	1–2 tbsp lemon juice
4 eggs	pinch of cayenne pepper
fresh flat-leaved parsley leaves,	salt and pepper
to garnish	225 g/8 oz unsalted butter, diced

NUTRITIONAL INFORMATION

Calories	.711
Protein	.18g
Carbohydrate	.18g
Sugars	.1g
Fat	.64g
Saturates	.37g

variation

For a cheat's version of Hollandaise sauce, heat 150 ml/5 fl oz double cream and 150 ml/5 fl oz mayonnaise, stirring constantly. Do not boil. Season.

cook's tip

When making Hollandaise sauce, if it becomes too thick, then slacken it with a little hot water. When the sauce is set over a saucepan of water, never let the water go above simmering point.

1 Preheat the grill to medium. To make the Hollandaise sauce, whisk the egg yolks with 1 tablespoon of the lemon juice, the cayenne pepper and salt and pepper to taste in a large, heavy-based saucepan. Add the butter and heat gently, whisking constantly, until the butter has melted and blended into the egg yolk. Remove the saucepan from the

heat and continue to whisk until the sauce is thick and creamy. Taste and add more lemon juice and seasoning, if necessary. Pour the sauce into a heatproof bowl and set over a saucepan of barely simmering water to keep warm.

2 Melt the butter in a frying pan over a low heat. Add the ham and cook,

turning occasionally, for 5 minutes, or until heated through. Toast the muffins under the preheated hot grill at the same time.

3 Meanwhile, bring a saucepan of water to the boil. Break an egg into a cup, stir the water to make a 'whirlpool' and slide in the egg. Poach for 3–4 minutes, or

until the white is set, but the yolk is soft. Remove and drain. Poach the remaining eggs in the same way.

4 Place a muffin half, cut-side up, on each of 4 warm plates. Top each with a slice of ham and an egg. Stir the Hollandaise sauce and spoon it over the eggs. Serve, garnished with parsley leaves.

stuffed tomatoes

serves 4 **prep: 10 mins** (L) **cook: 20 mins**

Tomatoes and anchovies taste wonderful together and make a delicious, light meal. Serve hot or warm in the Mediterranean style.

INGREDIENTS

4 large tomatoes

8 canned anchovy fillets, drained and finely chopped

25 g/1 oz fresh white breadcrumbs

1 garlic clove, finely chopped

1 tbsp olive oil

1 egg, lightly beaten

salt and pepper

crisp green salad, to serve

NUTRITIONAL INFORMATION	
Calories	100
Protein	5g
Carbohydrate	8g
Sugars	5g
Fat	6g
Saturates	1g

cook's tip

Beef tomatoes are ideal for filling as they are large and have a wonderful flavour. They should be ripe, but firm, to ensure that they hold their shape when stuffed and baked.

1 Preheat the oven to 190°C/375°F/Gas Mark 5. Using a sharp knife, slice the tops from the tomatoes and reserve. Scoop out the flesh with a teaspoon and reserve. Stand the tomato shells upside down on kitchen paper to drain.

2 Mix the anchovies, breadcrumbs, garlic, olive oil and enough of the egg to bind the mixture together in a small bowl. Season to taste with salt and pepper.

3 Spoon the filling into the tomato shells and replace the tops. Arrange the tomatoes in a large ovenproof dish and bake in the preheated oven for 20 minutes. Transfer to a large serving plate and serve hot or warm with a crisp green salad.

fried green tomatoes

⏱ **cook: 10 mins**　　　　⏱ **prep: 5 mins**　　　　**serves 4**

This crisp, golden savoury snack is ready in minutes, and undoubtedly deserves an Oscar for its performance.

NUTRITIONAL INFORMATION

Calories	.255
Protein	.6g
Carbohydrate	.33g
Sugars	.5g
Fat	.11g
Saturates	.2g

INGREDIENTS

115 g/4 oz coarse polenta

½ tsp garlic salt

1 tsp dried marjoram

2 tbsp plain flour

salt and pepper

1 egg

4 large green or slightly underripe
tomatoes, thickly sliced

sunflower oil, for deep-frying

cook's tip

Polenta is ground corn, and is also known as cornmeal. It is very popular in Italy and is available in several grades, from coarse to fine. Polenta is available in supermarkets and health food shops.

1 Place the polenta on a flat plate and stir in the garlic salt and marjoram. Place the flour on a second plate and season to taste with salt and pepper. Lightly beat the egg in a shallow bowl.

2 Dip the tomato slices first into the flour, then into the beaten egg and, finally, into the polenta to coat, then gently shake off any excess.

3 Pour the oil into a frying pan to a depth of 2.5 cm/1 inch and heat. Add the coated tomato slices, in batches, and fry, turning once, until golden and crisp. Keep warm while you cook the remaining slices. Transfer to a large serving plate and serve immediately.

indonesian sweetcorn balls

serves 4   **prep: 10 mins**   **cook: 10–15 mins**

These spicy little vegetable balls can be served hot or cold as a delicious snack or as one of several dishes to make up a complete Indonesian meal. They are also ideal for a buffet.

INGREDIENTS

115 g/4 oz unsalted peanuts

325 g/11½ oz canned sweetcorn, drained

1 onion, finely chopped

115 g/4 oz plain flour

1 tsp ground coriander

½ tsp sambal ulek or chilli sauce

salt

1–2 tbsp warm water (optional)

groundnut oil, for deep-frying

NUTRITIONAL INFORMATION

Calories	440
Protein	. . . . .13g
Carbohydrate	. . . . .49g
Sugars	. . . . .12g
Fat	. . . . .23g
Saturates	. . . . .4g

cook's tip

Sambal ulek is a fiery hot chilli sauce available from Asian food shops and supermarkets. If you cannot find it, then use chilli sauce instead.

1 Place the peanuts in a food processor and process briefly until coarsely ground. Alternatively, grind them in a mortar with a pestle. Transfer to a bowl and stir in the sweetcorn, onion, flour, coriander and sambal ulek. Season to taste with salt. Knead to a dough, adding a little warm water, if necessary, to make the dough workable.

2 Heat the oil in a deep-fryer or large, heavy-based saucepan. Using your hands, form tablespoonfuls of the dough into balls, then drop the sweetcorn balls into the hot oil, in batches, and cook until golden and crisp.

3 Remove the sweetcorn balls with a slotted spoon, drain on kitchen paper and keep warm while you cook the remaining batches. Serve immediately or leave to cool first.

peanut fritters

⏱ **cook: 10 mins**   ⏲ **prep: 5 mins**   **serves 4**

Popular with children and adults, these fritters are perfect for parties because they can be made in advance, stored in an airtight container, then reheated for 10 minutes in a medium–hot oven.

NUTRITIONAL INFORMATION	
Calories	.212
Protein	.5g
Carbohydrate	.15g
Sugars	.3g
Fat	.15g
Saturates	.3g

INGREDIENTS

55 g/2 oz rice flour
½ tsp baking powder
1 garlic clove, finely chopped
½ tsp ground turmeric
½ tsp ground coriander
⅛ tsp ground cumin
55 g/2 oz unsalted peanuts,
lightly crushed
125–150 ml/4–5 fl oz coconut milk
salt
groundnut oil, for frying

1 Place the rice flour, baking powder, garlic, turmeric, coriander, cumin and crushed peanuts together in a bowl and mix well. Gradually stir enough coconut milk into the mixture to make a smooth, thin batter. Season to taste with salt.

2 Pour the groundnut oil into a heavy-based frying pan to the depth of 1 cm/½ inch and heat.

3 Add spoonfuls of the batter to the frying pan, spacing them well apart, and cook until the tops have just set and the undersides are golden. Turn and cook for 1 minute, or until the second side is golden. Remove with a fish slice, drain on kitchen paper and keep warm while you cook the remaining fritters.

cook's tip

Coconut milk is not the same as the liquid found in the fresh nut. It is available in cans from supermarkets and Chinese food shops.

meat & poultry

Fast food has become a synonym for unhealthy, unappealing, rather boring and fairly tasteless meals, but the recipes featured here prove that this simply isn't true. They also show that you don't have to spend hours slaving over a hot stove to produce flavoursome, nourishing and imaginative dishes, whether for family meals or entertaining friends, weekend lunches or special occasions. Try Virginian Pork Chops (see page 129), served with peaches and a peppercorn sauce, or traditional Toad in the Hole with Onion Gravy (see page 144) for a midweek family supper; serve York Ham & Asparagus Rolls (see page 137) or Tarragon Chicken (see page 161) for an al fresco summer lunch; or impress at a dinner party with Tournedos Rossini (see page 125) or Butterflied Poussins (see page 168).

Even the most inexperienced or unenthusiastic cooks can have an international repertoire of fabulous dishes at their fingertips, from Beef Stroganoff (see page 122) to Chicken Teriyaki (see page 157). Recipes feature beef, pork, lamb, turkey and chicken – not to mention ham and sausages – and are grilled, braised, stir-fried and oven-cooked. From spicy and aromatic to rich and creamy, there is a dish to suit all tastes and occasions – and many take no more than 30 minutes from kitchen to table.

beef stroganoff

serves 4   **prep: 5 mins**   **cook: 12–15 mins**

Tender strips of steak are cooked in a creamy mushroom sauce to make a special meal in minutes.

INGREDIENTS

40 g/1½ oz plain flour

1 tsp paprika

salt and pepper

700 g/1 lb 9 oz rump steak, very thinly sliced into strips

55 g/2 oz butter

1 onion, finely chopped

1 garlic clove, finely chopped

225 g/8 oz button mushrooms

1 tbsp lemon juice

2 tbsp dry red wine

2 tbsp tomato purée

350 ml/12 fl oz soured cream

2 tbsp snipped fresh chives, to garnish

NUTRITIONAL INFORMATION

Calories	570
Protein	44g
Carbohydrate	16g
Sugars	7g
Fat	36g
Saturates	21g

cook's tip

If you have time, wrap the steak tightly in clingfilm and place in the freezer for 30 minutes. This will make it easier to slice wafer-thin.

1 Place the flour and paprika in a polythene bag and season with salt and pepper. Shake to mix, then add a few steak strips at a time and shake to coat.

2 Melt the butter in a large, heavy-based frying pan. Add the onion and garlic and cook over a low heat, stirring occasionally, for 5 minutes, or until softened. Increase the heat to high, add the steak strips and cook, stirring constantly, until browned all over. Stir in the mushrooms, lemon juice and wine, reduce the heat and simmer for 5 minutes.

3 Stir in the tomato purée and soured cream and adjust the seasoning, if necessary. Serve immediately, garnished with the chives.

beef kebabs

cook: 8 mins   prep: 15 mins   serves 4

This simple dish tastes wonderful and would make a delicious treat for any occasion. It would also be ideal for a barbecue party.

NUTRITIONAL INFORMATION	
Calories	335
Protein	40g
Carbohydrate	2g
Sugars	2g
Fat	19g
Saturates	4g

INGREDIENTS

8 spring onions

700 g/1 lb 9 oz rump steak,
cut into cubes

8 cherry tomatoes, halved

1 tbsp wholegrain mustard

1 tsp Worcestershire sauce

½ tsp balsamic vinegar

4 tbsp sunflower oil

salt and pepper

cook's tip

It is much quicker to use metal skewers for this dish because wooden ones need to be soaked in warm water for 30 minutes before using to prevent them burning under the grill or on the barbecue.

1 Preheat the grill to medium. Cut the spring onions into 10–13-cm/ 4–5-inch lengths and halve lengthways. Thread the steak cubes, spring onion lengths and cherry tomato halves alternately on to 4 wooden or metal skewers. Arrange them on a grill rack.

2 Mix the mustard, Worcestershire sauce and vinegar together in a small bowl. Whisk in the sunflower oil and season to taste with salt and pepper.

3 Brush the kebabs with the flavoured oil and cook under the preheated grill for 4 minutes. Turn over, brush with the flavoured oil again and cook for 4 minutes. Transfer to a large serving plate and serve immediately.

tournedos rossini

cook: 25 mins   **prep: 5 mins**   **serves 4**

NUTRITIONAL INFORMATION

Calories 607

Protein 33g

Carbohydrate 25g

Sugars 2g

Fat 39g

Saturates 21g

variation

Replace the shallot with a small, finely chopped onion and use chestnut mushrooms, which have a stronger flavour than button mushrooms.

Also known as filet mignon, tournedos is said to have got its name when a waiter, shocked by the composer Rossini asking for steak with foie gras and truffles, served the dish behind the backs of other customers. This is a rather less expensive, although still luxurious, version of the dish.

INGREDIENTS

4 slices fine chicken liver pâté

4 tournedos or round fillet steaks, about 2.5 cm/1 inch thick

115 g/4 oz butter

115 g/4 oz mushrooms, sliced

1 shallot, chopped

2 tbsp plain flour

425 ml/15 fl oz Beef Stock (see page 13)

125 ml/4 fl oz Madeira

salt and pepper

4 slices white bread, crusts removed

cook's tip

If you have time and would like a really tender cut of meat, then before cooking, place the steak between 2 sheets of clingfilm and, using a rolling pin or meat mallet, pound lightly.

1 Preheat the grill to medium. Cut the pâté to fit the top of the steaks and reserve. Melt 25 g/1 oz of the butter in a large frying pan. Add the mushrooms and cook over a low heat for 5 minutes, or until tender. Remove with a slotted spoon and reserve. Add the shallot to the frying pan and cook, stirring occasionally for 3–4 minutes, or until

softened. Sprinkle in the flour and cook, stirring constantly, for 1 minute. Remove the frying pan from the heat and gradually stir in the Beef Stock and Madeira.

2 Return the pan to the heat and bring to the boil, stirring constantly. Season to taste with salt and pepper, then simmer for 5 minutes.

3 Dot the steaks with 25 g/1 oz of the remaining butter and season to taste with pepper. Cook under the preheated grill for 4 minutes on each side, or according to taste. Meanwhile, to make the croûtons, melt the remaining butter in a separate heavy-based frying pan, add the bread and fry until golden brown on both sides.

4 Remove the steaks from the grill and keep warm. Place the slices of pâté in the juices in the grill pan and return to the grill to heat through. To serve, place a croûte on each of 4 warmed plates and top with the steak. Place a slice of pâté on top of each steak. Pour the grill pan juices into the sauce, sieve, stir in the mushrooms, then serve with the steaks.

steak in orange sauce

serves 4   **prep: 5 mins** ⟳   **cook: 6–8 mins** ⟲

This is a delightful dish for a special occasion. You can use fillet or sirloin steak, as both are very tender cuts.

INGREDIENTS

2 large oranges

25 g/1 oz butter

4 fillet steaks, about 175 g/6 oz each

salt and pepper

6 tbsp Beef Stock (see page 13)

1 tbsp balsamic vinegar

fresh flat-leaved parsley leaves, to garnish

NUTRITIONAL INFORMATION

Calories 330

Protein 38g

Carbohydrate 9g

Sugars 9g

Fat 16g

Saturates 8g

---

variation

Substitute 1 tablespoon Cointreau for 1 tablespoon of the orange juice in Step 1, if you prefer.

---

cook's tip

Balsamic vinegar comes from Modena in Italy and is the oldest and finest vinegar in the world. It is best used in simple dishes and in salad dressings. Balsamic vinegar is available from most large supermarkets.

1 Using a zester, pare a few strips of orange zest from 1 orange and reserve for the garnish. Cut the oranges in half, then cut off 4 thin slices and reserve for the garnish. Squeeze the juice from the remaining halves.

2 Melt the butter in a heavy-based frying pan. Add the steaks and cook over a medium heat for 1–2 minutes on each side, or until browned and sealed. Remove the steaks from the frying pan, season to taste with salt and pepper, reserve and keep warm.

3 Pour the orange juice into the frying pan and add the Beef Stock and vinegar. Simmer over a low heat for 2 minutes. Season the orange sauce to taste with salt and pepper and return the steaks to the frying pan. Heat through gently for 2 minutes, or according to taste. Transfer to warmed serving plates and garnish with the orange slices, orange zest and parsley leaves. Serve immediately.

virginian pork chops

⏲ **cook: 22 mins**   ⏱ **prep: 5 mins**   **serves 4**

NUTRITIONAL INFORMATION	
Calories	.557
Protein	.40g
Carbohydrate	.12g
Sugars	.11g
Fat	.39g
Saturates	.13g

variation

Substitute canned apricots for the peaches or use fresh fruit. Blanch, peel, stone and slice fresh peaches or nectarines; halve and stone apricots.

Succulent peaches balance the richness of pork, complementing chops superbly and creating a colourful dish.

INGREDIENTS

2 tbsp sunflower oil

4 pork chops, about 175 g/6 oz each

2 tbsp white wine

1 onion, chopped

415 g/14½ oz canned peach halves in natural juice, drained

1 tbsp pink or green peppercorns

150 ml/5 fl oz Chicken Stock (see page 13)

2–3 tsp balsamic vinegar

salt and pepper

cook's tip

Pink peppercorns are not a true pepper, but a processed berry from a South American tree. Green peppercorns are a true pepper. Buy freeze-dried or dehydrated peppercorns, not those in brine or vinegar.

1 Heat half the sunflower oil in a large, heavy-based frying pan. Add the chops and cook for 6 minutes on each side, or until browned and cooked through. Transfer to a plate, cover and keep warm. Pour off any excess fat from the frying pan and return to the heat. Add the wine and cook, for 2 minutes, stirring and scraping up any sediment from the base of the frying pan. Pour the liquid over the meat, re-cover and keep warm.

2 Wipe out the frying pan with kitchen paper and heat the remaining sunflower oil. Add the onion and cook over a low heat, stirring occasionally, for 5 minutes, or until softened. Meanwhile, slice the peach halves.

3 Add the peaches to the frying pan and heat through for 1 minute. Stir in the peppercorns, pour in the Chicken Stock and bring to simmering point. Return the chops and cooking juices to the frying pan and season to taste with vinegar, salt and pepper. Transfer to warmed plates and serve.

neapolitan pork steaks

serves 4   **prep: 10 mins** ⌛   **cook: 25 mins** ⌛

An Italian version of grilled pork steaks served with fresh vegetables, this dish is easy to make and delicious to eat.

INGREDIENTS

2 tbsp olive oil

1 large onion, sliced

1 garlic clove, chopped

400 g/14 oz canned tomatoes

2 tsp yeast extract

4 pork loin steaks, about
125 g/4½ oz each

75 g/2¾ oz black olives, stoned

2 tbsp fresh basil, shredded

freshly grated Parmesan cheese,
to garnish

green vegetables, to serve

NUTRITIONAL INFORMATION

Calories 353

Protein 39g

Carbohydrate 4g

Sugars 3g

Fat 20g

Saturates 5g

cook's tip

Parmesan is a mature and exceptionally hard cheese produced in Italy. You only need to add a little as it has a very strong flavour.

1 Preheat the grill to medium. Heat the oil in a large frying pan. Add the onion and garlic and cook, stirring, for 3–4 minutes, or until just beginning to soften.

2 Add the tomatoes and yeast extract to the frying pan and leave to simmer for 5 minutes, or until the sauce starts to thicken.

3 Cook the pork steaks, under the preheated grill, for 5 minutes on both sides, until the the meat is cooked through. Set the pork aside and keep warm.

4 Add the olives and shredded basil to the sauce in the frying pan and stir quickly to combine.

5 Transfer the steaks to warmed serving plates. Top with the sauce, garnish with freshly grated Parmesan cheese and serve immediately with green vegetables.

pork with fennel & juniper

cook: 15 mins

prep: 15 mins, plus 2 hrs marinating

serves 4

The addition of juniper and fennel to pork chops gives an unusual and delicate flavour to this dish.

NUTRITIONAL INFORMATION

Calories	.277
Protein	.32g
Carbohydrate	.0.4g
Sugars	.0.4g
Fat	.16g
Saturates	.5g

INGREDIENTS

½ fennel bulb

1 tbsp juniper berries

about 2 tbsp olive oil

finely grated rind and juice of 1 orange

4 pork chops, about 150 g/5½ oz each

TO SERVE

crisp salad

fresh bread

cook's tip

Juniper berries are commonly associated with gin, but they are often added to meat dishes in Italy for a delicate citrus flavour. They can be bought dried from health food shops and large supermarkets.

1 Finely chop the fennel bulb, discarding the green parts.

2 Grind the juniper berries in a pestle and mortar. Mix the crushed juniper berries with the fennel flesh, olive oil and orange rind.

3 Using a sharp knife, score a few cuts all over each pork chop. Place the chops in a roasting tin or ovenproof dish. Spoon the fennel and juniper mixture over the top. Pour over the orange juice, cover and leave to marinate in the refrigerator for about 2 hours.

4 Preheat the grill to medium. Cook the pork chops under the preheated grill for 10–15 minutes, depending on the thickness of the meat, or until the meat is tender and cooked through, turning occasionally.

5 Transfer the chops to serving plates and serve with a crisp, fresh salad and plenty of fresh bread to mop up the cooking juices.

pork stir-fry

serves 4   **prep: 15 mins** ⏲   **cook: 12 mins** ⏲

Stir-fries are always a popular choice for a midweek supper, as they introduce variety into the week's menus and are quick to cook.

INGREDIENTS

2 tbsp dark soy sauce

1 tbsp Chinese rice wine

1 tbsp Chinese rice vinegar

1 tbsp soft brown sugar

1 tsp Chinese five-spice powder

225 g/8 oz canned pineapple rings in juice

1 tbsp cornflour

1 tbsp groundnut oil

4 spring onions, chopped

1 garlic clove, finely chopped

2.5-cm/1-inch piece of fresh root ginger, finely chopped

350 g/12 oz pork loin, cut into very thin strips

3 carrots, cut into thin batons

175 g/6 oz baby corn cobs

1 green pepper, deseeded and cut into thin batons

115 g/4 oz beansprouts

115 g/4 oz mangetout

variation

Substitute the Chinese rice wine with the same amount of dry sherry and replace the mangetout with the same amount of sugar snap peas.

cook's tip

Chinese five-spice powder, which is different from the Indian blend, consists of Sichuan pepper, fennel, cloves, cinnamon and star anise.

1 Mix the soy sauce, rice wine, rice vinegar, sugar and five-spice powder together in a small bowl. Drain the pineapple, reserving the juice in a jug. Chop the pineapple and reserve until required. Stir the cornflour into the pineapple juice until a smooth paste forms, then stir the paste into the soy sauce mixture and reserve.

2 Heat the groundnut oil in a preheated wok or large, heavy-based frying pan. Add the spring onions, garlic and ginger and stir-fry for 30 seconds. Add the pork strips and stir-fry for 3 minutes, or until browned all over.

3 Add the carrots, baby corn cobs and green pepper and stir-fry for 3 minutes. Add the beansprouts and mangetout and stir-fry for 2 minutes. Add the pineapple and the soy sauce mixture and cook, stirring constantly, for a further 2 minutes, or until slightly thickened. Transfer to warmed serving bowls and serve immediately.

pork in creamy mushroom sauce

cook: 15 mins **prep: 10 mins** **serves 4**

NUTRITIONAL INFORMATION

Calories	.424
Protein	.40g
Carbohydrate	.3g
Sugars	.0g
Fat	.26g
Saturates	.14g

variation

If wild mushrooms are not available, use button mushrooms and add 25 g/ 1 oz dried porcini, soaked in hot water for 20 minutes then drained.

The perfect choice for easy entertaining, as the dish looks and tastes fabulous, but is actually astonishingly simple to prepare.

INGREDIENTS

25 g/1 oz unsalted butter

700 g/1 lb 9 oz pork loin, cut into thin strips

salt and pepper

280 g/10 oz mixed wild and cultivated mushrooms, halved, or quartered if large

6 tbsp dry white wine

225 ml/8 fl oz crème fraîche

1 tbsp chopped fresh sage

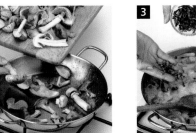

cook's tip

If possible, try to use fresh herbs as they have a much better flavour than dried. If they are not available, use freeze-dried herbs instead. These are found in most large supermarkets.

1 Melt the butter in a large, heavy-based frying pan. Add the pork strips and cook over a medium–low heat, stirring frequently, for 5 minutes, or until browned all over. Transfer to a plate with a slotted spoon, season to taste with salt and pepper, cover and keep warm.

2 Add the mushrooms to the frying pan and cook, stirring frequently, for 5–7 minutes, or until tender. Add the wine, bring to the boil and cook until reduced. Add the crème fraîche and return to the boil.

3 Return the pork to the frying pan, stir in the sage and heat through for 1–2 minutes. Transfer to a warmed serving dish and serve immediately.

gammon in madeira sauce

serves 4 **prep: 5 mins** **cook: 15 mins**

This is an easy version of an old-fashioned recipe that involves rather more time and effort. It is just as delicious. Serve with freshly cooked vegetables and potatoes for a tasty, nutritious supper.

INGREDIENTS

4 gammon steaks,
about 225 g/8 oz each

25 g/1 oz butter

2 cloves

1 mace blade

225 ml/8 fl oz Madeira

2 tsp Meaux mustard

fresh flat-leaved parsley sprigs,
to garnish

NUTRITIONAL INFORMATION	
Calories 493	
Protein 67g	
Carbohydrate 2g	
Sugars 2g	
Fat 18g	
Saturates 8g	

cook's tip

Mace is available in blades and ready ground. Try to buy blades, as the ground powder deteriorates rapidly. Store mace blades in a cool place in an airtight container.

1 Snip the edges of the gammon steaks with kitchen scissors to prevent them from curling up as they cook.

2 Melt the butter in a large, heavy-based frying pan, then add the cloves and mace blade. Add the gammon, in batches if necessary, and cook for 3 minutes on each side. Transfer to a warmed dish, cover and keep warm.

3 Add the Madeira to the frying pan and bring to the boil, stirring and scraping up any sediment from the base of the frying pan. Stir in the mustard and cook for 2 minutes, or until the sauce is thickened and glossy. Pour the sauce over the gammon, garnish with parsley sprigs and serve immediately.

york ham & asparagus rolls

⏱ **cook: 25 mins**   ◔ **prep: 5 mins**   **serves 6**

You can't really go wrong with a mixture of lean ham, asparagus and creamy cheese sauce. This dish makes a great main meal, but it can also be served as a starter for 8–10 people.

NUTRITIONAL INFORMATION

Calories	.464
Protein	.33g
Carbohydrate	.15g
Sugars	.7g
Fat	.31g
Saturates	.18g

INGREDIENTS

850 g/1 lb 14 oz canned asparagus spears, drained

12 slices cooked York ham

CHEESE SAUCE

55 g/2 oz butter

55 g/2 oz plain flour

600 ml/1 pint milk

1 tbsp Dijon mustard

140 g/5 oz Cheddar cheese, grated

150 g/5½ oz Gruyère cheese, grated

pinch of freshly grated nutmeg

salt and pepper

cook's tip

York ham is one of the British hams that is still preserved by the old traditional methods. Suffolk ham is another fine British ham.

1 Preheat the oven to 180°C/350°F/Gas Mark 4. To make the sauce, melt the butter in a large, heavy-based saucepan. Sprinkle in the flour and cook, stirring constantly, for 1 minute. Remove the saucepan from the heat and gradually whisk in the milk. Return the saucepan to the heat and bring to the boil, stirring constantly. Cook until smooth and thickened, then remove from the heat and stir in the mustard, Cheddar and Gruyère cheese. Season to taste with nutmeg, salt and pepper.

2 Divide the asparagus spears equally between the slices of ham. Roll up the ham and place, seam-side down, in a large ovenproof dish. Pour the cheese sauce over the ham rolls.

3 Bake in the preheated oven for 20 minutes. Serve immediately.

spanish cutlets

serves 4   **prep: 5 mins** ⟳   **cook: 25 mins** ⟳

Peppers, tomatoes, olives and fresh herbs add colour, flavour and interest to this simple dish of braised lamb cutlets.

INGREDIENTS

1 tbsp olive oil	400 g/14 oz canned chopped tomatoes
1 onion, sliced	2 tsp chopped fresh thyme
1 garlic clove, finely chopped	1 tsp chopped fresh rosemary
2 red peppers, deseeded and sliced	2 tbsp black olives
8 lamb cutlets, trimmed of excess fat	salt and pepper

NUTRITIONAL INFORMATION

Calories	.465
Protein	.17g
Carbohydrate	.9g
Sugars	.8g
Fat	.40g
Saturates	.19g

variation

Substitute the red peppers with yellow or orange peppers and replace the onion with a red onion, if you prefer.

cook's tip

You can buy olives that have already been stoned from most supermarkets, although try not to buy those stored in brine as they may make the finished dish too salty.

1 Heat the olive oil in a large, heavy-based frying pan. Add the onion, garlic and red peppers and cook over a low heat, stirring occasionally, for 5 minutes, or until softened.

2 Increase the heat to medium, add the lamb cutlets and cook for 1–2 minutes on each side, or until browned.

3 Add the chopped tomatoes, thyme and rosemary, then cover and simmer for 15 minutes, or until the lamb is tender. Stir in the olives, season to taste with salt and pepper and serve immediately, straight from the frying pan.

lamb with olives

serves 4 **prep: 15 mins** **cook: 1 hr 30 mins**

This is a very simple dish, and the chilli adds a bit of spiciness. It is quick to prepare and makes an ideal supper dish.

INGREDIENTS

1.25 kg/2 lb 12 oz boned leg of lamb
6 tbsp olive oil
2 garlic cloves, crushed
1 onion, sliced
1 small red chilli, cored, deseeded and finely chopped
175 ml/6 fl oz dry white wine
175 g/6 oz stoned black olives
salt
fresh parsley sprigs, to garnish
crusty bread, to serve

NUTRITIONAL INFORMATION

Calories	.577
Protein	.62g
Carbohydrate	.1g
Sugars	.1g
Fat	.33g
Saturates	.10g

variation

You could garnish this dish with fresh coriander instead of parsley. Serve with warm ciabatta or focaccia instead of plain bread, if you like.

1 Preheat the oven to 180°C/350°F/Gas Mark 4. Using a sharp knife, cut the lamb into 2.5-cm/ 1-inch cubes.

2 Heat the oil in a frying pan, add the garlic, onion and chilli and cook for 5 minutes. Add the meat and wine and cook for a further 5 minutes.

3 Stir in the olives, then transfer the mixture to a casserole. Bake in the preheated oven for 1 hour 20 minutes, or until the meat is tender. Season with salt to taste, garnish with chopped fresh parsley and serve.

lamb with bay & lemon

cook: 35 mins   **prep: 10 mins**   serves 4

These lamb chops quickly become more elegant and sophisticated when the bone is removed to make small, tender noisettes.

NUTRITIONAL INFORMATION	
Calories	268
Protein	. . . . .24g
Carbohydrate	. . . . .0.2g
Sugars	. . . . .0.2g
Fat	. . . . .16g
Saturates	. . . . .7g

INGREDIENTS

4 lamb chops

1 tbsp olive oil

15 g/½ oz butter

150 ml/5 fl oz white wine

150 ml/5 fl oz lamb or Vegetable Stock (see page 13)

2 bay leaves

pared rind of 1 lemon

salt and pepper

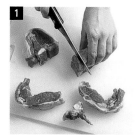  

cook's tip

Your local butcher will offer you good advice on how to prepare the lamb noisettes if you have not prepared them before.

1 Using a sharp knife, carefully remove the bone from each lamb chop, keeping the meat intact. Shape the meat into rounds and secure with a length of string. Alternatively, ask your butcher to prepare the noisettes.

2 Place the oil and butter in a large frying pan and heat until the mixture starts to froth. Add the noisettes to the pan and cook for 2–3 minutes on each side, or until browned. Remove the pan from the heat and drain off and discard the excess fat.

3 Return the frying pan to the heat. Add the wine, stock, bay leaves and lemon rind and cook for 20–25 minutes, or until the lamb is tender. Season the lamb noisettes and sauce with salt and pepper to taste.

4 Transfer to serving plates. Remove the string from each noisette and serve with the cooking sauce.

stir-fried lamb

🕛 **cook: 15 mins** 　　　 🕒 **prep: 10 mins** 　　　 **serves 4**

Lamb is a less popular choice for stir-frying than beef or pork, yet it works very well, as this mint-flavoured medley of neck fillet and crisp vegetables demonstrates.

INGREDIENTS

4 tbsp groundnut oil	350 g/12 oz fresh spinach leaves
550 g/1 lb 4 oz neck fillet of lamb, thinly sliced	2 tbsp lime juice
	3 tbsp oyster sauce
1 large onion, finely chopped	2 tbsp Thai fish sauce
2 garlic cloves, finely chopped	2 tsp caster sugar
2 fresh red chillies, deseeded and thinly sliced	5 tbsp chopped fresh mint
	salt and pepper
175 g/6 oz mangetout	

variation

Replace the lime juice with the same amount of lemon juice and if you don't like it too spicy, use just 1 fresh red chilli.

cook's tip

Oyster sauce is a thick soy sauce, which is flavoured with oyster juice. The flavour is very delicate and is ideal for dishes that need livening up. It is found in most supermarkets and Chinese food shops.

1 Heat the groundnut oil in a preheated wok or large, heavy-based frying pan. Add the lamb and stir-fry over a high heat for 2–3 minutes, or until browned all over. Remove with a slotted spoon and drain on kitchen paper.

2 Add the onion, garlic and chillies to the wok and stir-fry for 3 minutes. Add the mangetout and stir-fry for 2 minutes, then stir in the spinach leaves and return the lamb to the wok.

3 Add the lime juice, oyster sauce, Thai fish sauce and sugar and cook, stirring constantly, for 4 minutes, or until the lamb is cooked through and tender. Stir in the chopped mint, season to taste with salt and pepper and serve immediately.

toad in the hole with onion gravy

serves 4   **prep: 5 mins** ⏱   **cook: 20 mins** ⏱

This traditional English dish was originally made with pieces of cooked meat and bacon. Nowadays, pork sausages are used. The ends of each sausage stick out of the surrounding Yorkshire pudding batter like a toad poking its head out of a hole.

INGREDIENTS

8 pork sausages

25 g/1 oz dripping or lard or

2 tbsp vegetable oil

3 eggs

salt and pepper

300 ml/10 fl oz milk

115 g/4 oz plain flour

ONION GRAVY

2 tbsp sunflower oil

1 onion, chopped

1 tbsp plain flour

200 ml/7 fl oz Chicken Stock

(see page 13)

1 tsp red wine vinegar

salt and pepper

NUTRITIONAL INFORMATION

Calories 780

Protein 23g

Carbohydrate 44g

Sugars 8g

Fat 58g

Saturates 21g

variation

For extra-crisp batter, replace half the milk with water, and for extra flavour, stir in 1 teaspoon dried thyme.

cook's tip

Switch on the oven to preheat before you so much as wash your hands. It is essential that the oven and the muffin tray are very hot before you bake the batter.

1 Preheat the oven to 230°C/450°F/Gas Mark 8. Using kitchen scissors, cut in between the sausages to separate them, spread them out on a baking sheet and partially cook in the preheated oven for 10 minutes, while you make the batter. Grease the cups of a muffin tray with the dripping, and place in the oven to heat up at the same time.

2 Using a balloon whisk, lightly beat the eggs with salt and pepper to taste in a small bowl, then add half the milk. Sift the flour into a large bowl, add the egg mixture and stir until a smooth batter forms. Stir in the remaining milk. Remove the sausages and muffin tray from the oven and place 2 sausages in each cup. Pour in the batter and return

to the oven for 10 minutes, or until the batter is puffed up and golden.

3 Meanwhile, make the onion gravy. Heat the oil in a large saucepan, add the onion and cook over a low heat, stirring occasionally, for 5 minutes, or until softened. Sprinkle in the flour and cook, stirring, for 1 minute. Remove

the saucepan from the heat and gradually stir in the Chicken Stock.

4 Return to the heat and bring to the boil, stirring constantly. Stir in the vinegar and season to taste with salt and pepper. Remove the toad in the hole from the oven and serve, handing the gravy separately.

fresh spaghetti & meatballs

serves 4   **prep: 45 mins** ☾   **cook: 1 hr 15 mins** ☾

*This well-loved Italian dish is famous across the world. Make the
most of it by using high-quality steak for the meatballs.*

INGREDIENTS

150 g/5½ oz brown breadcrumbs	1 tbsp finely chopped fresh tarragon
150 ml/5 fl oz milk	salt and pepper
25 g/1 oz butter	1 large onion, chopped
25 g/1 oz wholemeal flour	450 g/1 lb minced steak
200 ml/7 fl oz Beef Stock (see page 13)	1 tsp paprika
400 g/14 oz canned chopped tomatoes	4 tbsp olive oil
2 tbsp tomato purée	450 g/1 lb fresh spaghetti
1 tsp sugar	fresh tarragon leaves, to garnish

NUTRITIONAL INFORMATION

Calories	665
Protein	. . . . .39g
Carbohydrate	. . . . .77g
Sugars	. . . . .9g
Fat	. . . . .24g
Saturates	. . . . .8g

variation

You can use skinned, chopped fresh
tomatoes instead of canned tomatoes,
but add an extra tablespoon of tomato
purée to boost their flavour.

cook's tip

Fresh spaghetti cooks very
quickly when placed straight
into boiling water. Be careful
not to overcook it, otherwise
it will taste sticky and heavy.

1 Place the breadcrumbs
in a bowl, add the milk
and set aside to soak for about
30 minutes.

2 Melt half of the butter
in a pan. Add the flour
and cook, stirring constantly,
for 2 minutes. Gradually stir in
the Beef Stock and cook,
stirring constantly, for a further
5 minutes. Add the tomatoes,
tomato purée, sugar and
tarragon. Season well and
simmer for 25 minutes.

3 Preheat the oven
to 180°C/350°F/Gas
Mark 4. Mix the onion,
steak and paprika into the
breadcrumbs and season
to taste with salt and pepper.
Shape the mixture into
14 meatballs.

4 Heat the oil and
remaining butter in a
frying pan, add the meatballs
and cook, turning, until
browned. Place in a deep
casserole, pour over the tomato
sauce, cover and bake in the
preheated oven for 25 minutes.

5 Bring a large saucepan
of lightly salted water
to the boil. Add the spaghetti,
bring back to the boil and
cook for 2–3 minutes, or until
tender but still firm to the bite.

6 Meanwhile, remove
the meatballs from
the oven. Leave to cool for
3 minutes. Serve the meatballs
and sauce on top of the
spaghetti, garnished with
tarragon leaves.

neapolitan veal cutlets

serves 4   **prep: 20 mins** (⏱)   **cook: 45 mins** (⏱)

*The delicious combination of apple, onion and mushrooms
perfectly complements the delicate flavour of veal.*

INGREDIENTS

200 g/7 oz butter	1 tbsp sesame seeds
4 veal cutlets, about 250 g/9 oz	salt and pepper
each, trimmed	400 g/14 oz dried marille
1 large onion, sliced	100 ml/3½ fl oz extra virgin olive oil
2 apples, peeled, cored and sliced	175 g/6 oz mascarpone cheese
175 g/6 oz button mushrooms	2 large beef tomatoes, cut in half
1 tbsp chopped fresh tarragon	leaves of 1 fresh basil sprig, plus
8 black peppercorns	a few leaves, to garnish

NUTRITIONAL INFORMATION

Calories	1071
Protein	74g
Carbohydrate	66g
Sugars	13g
Fat	59g
Saturates	16g

variation

You can also use tagliatelle or tagliarini for this dish. If you like, replace the mascarpone cheese with sour cream.

cook's tip

Use eating apples such as Cox's or Braeburn apples for this dish. You can place the sliced apples in cold water with a little lemon juice added to prevent them from going brown before cooking.

1 Preheat the oven to 150°C/300°F/Gas Mark 2. Place 2 ovenproof dishes in the oven to warm. Melt 55 g/2 oz of the butter in a frying pan. Add the veal and cook over a low heat for 5 minutes on each side. Transfer to a warmed ovenproof dish and place in the oven to keep warm. Add the onion and apples to the pan and cook until lightly browned. Transfer to the other ovenproof dish, place the veal on top and keep warm.

2 Melt the remaining butter in the frying pan. Add the mushrooms, tarragon and peppercorns and cook gently over a low heat for 3 minutes. Sprinkle over the sesame seeds.

3 Preheat the grill to medium. Bring a pan of salted water to the boil. Add the pasta and 1 tablespoon of the oil. Cook for 8–10 minutes, until tender but firm to the bite. Meanwhile, grill the tomatoes and basil for 2–3 minutes.

4 Drain the pasta and transfer to a serving plate. Spoon the mascarpone on top and sprinkle over the remaining olive oil. Place the onions, apples and veal cutlets on top of the pasta. Spoon the mushrooms, peppercorns and pan juices on to the cutlets, place the tomatoes and basil leaves around the edge and bake in the preheated oven for 5 minutes. Season to taste, garnish with fresh basil leaves and serve immediately.

veal italienne

serves 4   **prep: 25 mins** ⟳   **cook: 1 hr 20 mins** ⟳

This dish is really superb if made with tender veal. However, if veal is unavailable, use pork or turkey escalopes instead.

INGREDIENTS

55 g/2 oz butter

1 tbsp olive oil

675 g/1½ lb potatoes, cubed

4 veal escalopes, about 175 g/6 oz each

1 onion, cut into 8 wedges

2 garlic cloves, crushed

2 tbsp plain flour

2 tbsp tomato purée

150 ml/5 fl oz red wine

300 ml/10 fl oz Chicken Stock (see page 13)

8 ripe tomatoes, peeled, deseeded and diced

25 g/1 oz stoned black olives, halved

2 tbsp chopped fresh basil, plus a few leaves, to garnish

salt and pepper

NUTRITIONAL INFORMATION	
Calories	.592
Protein	.44g
Carbohydrate	.48g
Sugars	.5g
Fat	.23g
Saturates	.9g

variation

To save time, you can substitute 400 g/14 oz canned chopped tomatoes for the fresh tomatoes.

cook's tip

For a quicker cooking time and really tender meat, pound the veal with a meat mallet to flatten it slightly before you begin cooking.

1 Preheat the oven to 180°C/350°F/Gas Mark 4. Heat the butter and oil in a large frying pan. Add the potato cubes and cook for 5–7 minutes, stirring frequently, until beginning to brown. Remove the potatoes from the pan with a slotted spoon and set aside.

2 Place the veal in the frying pan and cook for 2–3 minutes on each side, until sealed. Remove from the pan and set aside.

3 Add the onion and garlic to the pan and cook for 2–3 minutes. Add the flour and tomato purée and cook for 1 minute, stirring. Gradually blend in the red wine and Stock, stirring to make a smooth sauce.

4 Return the potatoes and veal to the pan. Stir in the tomatoes, olives and chopped basil and season with salt and pepper.

5 Transfer to a casserole and cook in the preheated oven for 1 hour, or until the potatoes and veal are cooked through. Garnish with basil leaves and serve.

veal in a rose petal sauce

serves 4   **prep: 10 mins** ⏲   **cook: 35 mins** ⏱

This truly spectacular dish is equally delicious whether you use veal or pork fillet. Make sure the roses are free of blemishes and pesticides.

INGREDIENTS

450 g/1 lb dried fettuccine

100 ml/3½ fl oz olive oil

1 tsp chopped fresh oregano

1 tsp chopped fresh marjoram

175 g/6 oz butter

450 g/1 lb veal fillet, thinly sliced

150 ml/5 fl oz rose petal vinegar
(see Cook's Tip)

150 ml/5 fl oz fish stock

50 ml/2 fl oz grapefruit juice

50 ml/2 fl oz double cream

salt

TO GARNISH

12 pink grapefruit segments

12 pink peppercorns

rose petals, washed

fresh herb leaves

NUTRITIONAL INFORMATION

Calories 810

Protein 31g

Carbohydrate 49g

Sugars 2g

Fat 56g

Saturates 28g

variation

This dish also tastes good served with fresh tagliatelle or tagliarini, which can be cooked while the veal is cooking in Step 2.

cook's tip

To make the rose petal vinegar, infuse the petals of 8 pesticide-free roses in 150 ml/5 fl oz white wine vinegar for 48 hours. Make this well in advance to reduce the preparation time.

1 Bring a large saucepan of lightly salted water to the boil. Add the fettuccine and 1 tablespoon of the oil and cook for 8–10 minutes, or until tender but still firm to the bite. Drain and transfer to a warmed serving dish, sprinkle over 2 tablespoons of the olive oil, the oregano and the marjoram. Keep warm.

2 Heat 50 g/2 oz of the butter with the remaining oil in a large frying pan. Add the veal and cook over a low heat for 6 minutes. Remove the veal from the pan and place on top of the pasta.

3 Add the vinegar and fish stock to the pan and bring to the boil. Boil vigorously until reduced by two thirds. Add the grapefruit juice and cream and simmer over a low heat for 4 minutes. Dice the remaining butter and add to the pan, one piece at a time, whisking constantly until completely incorporated.

4 Pour the sauce around the veal, then garnish with the pink grapefruit segments, pink peppercorns and rose petals. Scatter over your favourite herb leaves and serve.

turkey breasts with orange sauce

cook: 10 mins   **prep: 10 mins**   **serves 4**

NUTRITIONAL INFORMATION

Calories 300

Protein 34g

Carbohydrate 1g

Sugars 1g

Fat 18g

Saturates 9g

variation

To make a lemon sauce, simply substitute lemon juice for the orange juice, lemon slices for the orange slices and lemon balm for the chervil.

This is a fragrant, summery dish that needs nothing more than a crisp salad and fresh rolls to make a satisfying supper.

INGREDIENTS

4 turkey breast steaks,
about 140 g/5 oz each
salt and pepper
55 g/2 oz butter
2 tbsp olive oil
6 tbsp Chicken Stock (see page 13)
3–4 tbsp orange juice
1 tbsp chopped fresh chervil

TO GARNISH
orange slices
fresh chervil sprigs

cook's tip

Blood oranges are a good choice for this dish, as they are very juicy and have a sharp edge to their flavour. If you cannot find blood oranges, then use ordinary ones instead.

1 Place each turkey breast steak in turn between 2 sheets of clingfilm and beat with the side of a rolling pin or the flat surface of a meat mallet until about 5 mm/ $1/4$ inch thick. Season to taste with salt and pepper.

2 Melt half the butter with the oil in a large, griddle pan. Add half the turkey steaks and cook over a high heat, turning once, for 3–4 minutes, or until lightly browned on both sides. Remove from the griddle pan, add the remaining turkey steaks, 1 at a time, and cook in the same way. Keep warm.

3 Pour the Chicken Stock into the griddle pan and bring to the boil, stirring and scraping up any sediment from the base of the pan. Add 3 tablespoons of the orange juice, the remaining butter and the chervil, then reduce the heat to a simmer.

4 Return all the turkey steaks, with any meat juices, to the griddle pan. Simmer gently for 1 minute on each side. Taste and adjust the seasoning, adding more orange juice if necessary. Serve immediately, garnished with orange slices and chervil sprigs.

chicken cordon bleu

serves 4 **prep: 5 mins** ☾ **cook: 25 mins** ⏱

Once extremely trendy and popular, this dish has rather gone out of fashion, which is a shame because it has a lovely flavour and texture, as well as being simplicity itself to prepare.

INGREDIENTS

4 skinless, boneless chicken breasts, about 140 g/5 oz each

4 slices cooked ham

4 tbsp grated Gruyère cheese

salt and pepper

2 tbsp olive oil

115 g/4 oz button mushrooms, sliced

4 tbsp dry white wine

NUTRITIONAL INFORMATION

Calories	.300
Protein	.40g
Carbohydrate	.1g
Sugars	.1g
Fat	.15g
Saturates	.5g

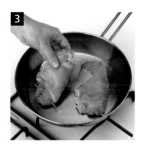

variation

Substitute 115 g/4 oz thinly sliced ricotta cheese for the Gruyère cheese and replace the button mushrooms with chestnut mushrooms.

1 Place each chicken breast in turn between 2 sheets of clingfilm and beat with the side of a rolling pin or the flat surface of a meat mallet until about 5 mm/¼ inch thick.

2 Lay a slice of ham on each chicken breast and sprinkle 1 tablespoon of the Gruyère cheese over half of each slice. Season to taste with salt and pepper. Fold the chicken over and secure with wooden cocktail sticks.

3 Heat the olive oil in a large, heavy-based frying pan. Add the chicken and cook over a high heat for 2–3 minutes on each side, or until golden brown all over. Remove from the frying pan and keep warm. Add the mushrooms to the frying pan and cook, stirring frequently, for 2–3 minutes, or until browned, then return the chicken to the frying pan and pour in the wine.

4 Reduce the heat and simmer for 15 minutes, or until the chicken is tender and cooked through. Remove and discard the cocktail sticks and serve the chicken with the mushrooms.

chicken teriyaki

cook: 15 mins　　　**prep: 15 mins**　　　**serves 4**

This Japanese-style stir-fry is full of flavour, although it is marinated for only a brief time. To create an authentic flavour, it is best to use tamari – Japanese soy sauce – if available.

NUTRITIONAL INFORMATION

Calories 348

Protein 29g

Carbohydrate 51g

Sugars 1g

Fat 4g

Saturates 1g

INGREDIENTS

450 g/1 lb skinless, boneless chicken

breasts, thinly sliced into strips

2 tbsp tamari or dark soy sauce

1 tbsp Chinese rice wine

1 tbsp dry sherry

1 tsp sugar

grated rind of 1 orange

225 g/8 oz long-grain rice

500 ml/18 fl oz water

pinch of salt

cook's tip

When marinating chicken, it is best to cover with clingfilm and leave to marinate in the refrigerator. If a stronger flavour is needed and you have time, leave it to marinate for 2 hours, turning occasionally.

1 Place the chicken strips in a large, shallow dish. Mix the tamari, rice wine, sherry, sugar and orange rind together in a jug, stirring until the sugar has dissolved. Pour the marinade over the chicken, stir to coat and leave to marinate for 15 minutes.

2 Meanwhile, place the rice in a large, heavy-based saucepan. Pour in the water, add the salt and bring to the boil. Stir once, reduce the heat, cover tightly and simmer very gently for 10 minutes. Remove the saucepan from the heat, but do not remove the lid.

3 Heat a wok or large, heavy-based frying pan. Add the chicken and the marinade and cook, stirring constantly, for 5 minutes, or until the chicken is cooked through and tender. Remove the lid from the rice and fork through the grains to fluff up, then serve immediately with the chicken.

chinese chicken

serves 4 **prep: 10 mins** ⟳ **cook: 4 mins** ⏲

As in all Chinese dishes, the matching and contrasting flavours, colours and textures in this tempting Eastern recipe produce a harmonious – and utterly delicious – result.

INGREDIENTS

280 g/10 oz skinless, boneless chicken breasts, very thinly sliced	8 shiitake mushrooms, halved if large
¼ tsp cornflour	115 g/4 oz canned bamboo shoots, drained and rinsed
1¼ tsp water	1 tsp finely chopped fresh root ginger
1 small egg white, lightly beaten	1 tbsp dark soy sauce
salt	1 tbsp Chinese rice wine or dry sherry
4 tbsp groundnut oil	1 tsp light brown sugar
2 spring onions, cut into short lengths	dash of sesame oil
115 g/4 oz green beans, halved	

NUTRITIONAL INFORMATION

Calories 214

Protein 18g

Carbohydrate 4g

Sugars 2g

Fat 14g

Saturates 3g

variation

Substitute the shiitake mushrooms with wild mushrooms, such as chanterelles, if you like.

cook's tip

Sesame oil is widely used in Chinese and Asian dishes. It is usually used as a flavouring at the end of cooking as it burns very easily.

1 Cut the chicken slices into small pieces and place in a bowl. Mix the cornflour and water together until a smooth paste forms and add to the chicken with the egg white and a pinch of salt. Stir well to coat.

2 Heat the groundnut oil in a preheated wok or large, heavy-based frying pan.

Add the chicken and stir-fry over a medium heat for 45 seconds, or until browned. Remove from the wok with a slotted spoon.

3 Increase the heat to high, add the spring onions, green beans, mushrooms, bamboo shoots and ginger and stir-fry for 1 minute. Return the chicken

to the wok. Mix the soy sauce and rice wine together in a small jug and add to the wok with the sugar and a pinch of salt. Cook, stirring constantly, for a further 1 minute. Sprinkle with a dash of sesame oil and serve immediately.

honey-glazed chicken

serves 4   **prep: 5 mins** ☾   **cook: 20 mins** ⏱

This sherry-flavoured honey glaze can be brushed on to any cuts of chicken – thighs are used here – before grilling or cooking on the barbecue. The honey brings out the flavour of the meat.

INGREDIENTS

8 skinless chicken thighs

salt

GLAZE

250 ml/9 fl oz medium sherry

1 tbsp cornflour

3 tbsp clear honey

3 tbsp red wine vinegar

1 tbsp dark soy sauce

3 garlic cloves, finely chopped

NUTRITIONAL INFORMATION

Calories 300

Protein 23g

Carbohydrate 24g

Sugars 16g

Fat 6g

Saturates 2g

1 Preheat the grill to medium. To make the glaze, pour 225 ml/8 fl oz of the sherry into a small saucepan and bring to the boil. Continue to boil for 6 minutes, or until reduced by half. Meanwhile, mix the remaining sherry and cornflour together in a small bowl until a smooth paste forms.

2 Remove the sherry from the heat and whisk in the honey, vinegar, soy sauce and garlic. Return the saucepan to the heat and whisk in the cornflour paste. Simmer, whisking constantly, for 1 minute, then remove from the heat and leave to cool slightly.

3 Season the chicken thighs with salt and place them on a grill rack. Brush generously with the glaze and cook under the preheated grill for 7 minutes.

4 Turn the chicken thighs over, brush generously with the glaze and grill for a further 3–4 minutes, or until the chicken is completely cooked through and tender. Transfer to warmed serving plates and serve immediately.

cook's tip

If the juices run clear and not pink when the thickest part of the chicken is pierced with a skewer or the point of a knife, it is cooked through.

tarragon chicken

⏱ **cook: 20 mins**   ◔ **prep: 5 mins**   **serves 4**

This is a classic French recipe and it is such a stylish, yet understated dish that it would be an excellent choice for a main course at an informal dinner party.

NUTRITIONAL INFORMATION	
Calories	.420
Protein	.39g
Carbohydrate	.2g
Sugars	.1g
Fat	.27g
Saturates	.15g

INGREDIENTS

4 skinless, boneless chicken breasts, about 175 g/6 oz each

salt and pepper

125 ml/4 fl oz dry white wine

225–300 ml/8–10 fl oz Chicken Stock (see page 13)

1 garlic clove, finely chopped

1 tbsp dried tarragon

175 ml/6 fl oz double cream

1 tbsp chopped fresh tarragon

fresh tarragon sprigs, to garnish

cook's tip

Tongs are the easiest way to remove the chicken breasts from the frying pan. Make sure that the chicken is completely cooked through before serving.

1 Season the chicken with salt and pepper and place in a single layer in a large, heavy-based frying pan. Pour in the wine and enough Chicken Stock just to cover and add the garlic and dried tarragon. Bring to the boil, reduce the heat and poach gently for 10 minutes, or until the chicken is cooked through and tender.

2 Remove the chicken with a slotted spoon or tongs, cover and keep warm. Sieve the poaching liquid into a clean frying pan and skim off any fat from the surface. Bring to the boil and cook until reduced by about two-thirds.

3 Stir in the cream, return to the boil and cook until reduced by about half.

Stir in the fresh tarragon. Slice the chicken breasts and arrange on warmed plates. Spoon over the sauce, garnish with tarragon sprigs and serve immediately.

chicken braised in red wine

cook: 27 mins   **prep: 2 mins**   **serves 4**

NUTRITIONAL INFORMATION

Calories 423

Protein 41g

Carbohydrate 8g

Sugars 7g

Fat 20g

Saturates 5g

Rich in colour and flavour, this dish needs little in the way of accompaniments except some fresh rustic bread, a little green salad and a glass of the same red wine.

INGREDIENTS

3 tbsp olive oil	300 ml/10 fl oz full-bodied red wine
4 skinless, boneless chicken breasts,	300 ml/10 fl oz Chicken Stock
about 140 g/5 oz each	(see page 13) or water
1 red onion, halved and sliced	salt and pepper
2 tbsp red pesto	115 g/4 oz seedless red grapes, halved

variation

You can use other cuts of chicken, such as drumsticks and thighs, but meat on the bone may need slightly longer cooking in Step 3.

cook's tip

If time is short, cut the chicken into small strips or cubes, cook over a medium heat in Step 1 until cooked through and omit the simmering time in Step 3. Make sure the chicken is piping hot before serving.

1 Heat 2 tablespoons of the olive oil in a large, heavy-based frying pan or flameproof casserole. Add the chicken and cook over a medium heat for 3 minutes on each side, or until golden. Remove from the frying pan and reserve until required.

2 Add the remaining olive oil to the frying pan. When it is hot, add the onion and pesto and cook over a low heat, stirring occasionally, for 5 minutes, or until the onion is softened. Pour in the wine and Chicken Stock and bring to the boil, stirring constantly.

3 Return the chicken to the frying pan, season to taste with salt and pepper, cover and simmer for 15 minutes, or until the chicken is tender. Add the grapes and heat through for 1 minute. Transfer to warmed dishes and serve immediately.

chicken with green olives

serves 4   **prep: 15 mins**   **cook: 1 hr 30 mins**

Olives are a popular flavouring for poultry and game in the Apulia region of Italy, where this traditional recipe originates.

INGREDIENTS

3 tbsp olive oil

25 g/1 oz butter

4 chicken breasts, part boned

1 large onion, finely chopped

2 garlic cloves, crushed

2 red peppers, cored, deseeded and cut into large pieces

250 g/9 oz button mushrooms, sliced or quartered

175 g/6 oz tomatoes, skinned and halved

150 ml/5 fl oz dry white wine

175 g/6 oz stoned green olives

4–6 tbsp double cream

400 g/14 oz dried farfalle

salt and pepper

chopped flat-leaved parsley, to garnish

NUTRITIONAL INFORMATION

Calories 614

Protein 34g

Carbohydrate 49g

Sugars 6g

Fat 30g

Saturates 11g

variation

Add a little extra colour to this dish by using green and yellow peppers instead of the red peppers.

cook's tip

Skin the tomatoes by placing them in a bowl and pouring boiling water from the kettle over them. Leave to stand for 1 minute, then drain and cool under cold running water. The skins should come off easily.

1 Preheat the oven to 180°C/350°F/Gas Mark 4. Place 2 tablespoons of the oil and the butter in a frying pan over a medium heat. Add the chicken breasts and cook for 3–4 minutes, until golden brown all over. Remove the chicken from the pan.

2 Add the onion and garlic to the pan and cook for 1–2 minutes, until beginning to soften. Add the peppers and mushrooms and cook for 2–3 minutes. Add the tomatoes and season to taste with salt and pepper. Transfer the vegetable mixture to a casserole and arrange the chicken on top.

3 Add the wine to the pan and bring to the boil. Pour the wine over the chicken. Cover and bake in the preheated oven for 50 minutes.

4 Add the olives to the casserole and mix in. Pour in the cream, cover and return to the oven for 10–20 minutes.

5 Meanwhile, bring a pan of lightly salted water to the boil. Add the pasta and the remaining oil and cook for 8–10 minutes, or until tender but still firm to the bite. Drain and transfer to a serving dish.

6 Serve the chicken and its sauce with the pasta, garnished with parsley.

garlic & herb chicken

serves 4   **prep: 20 mins** ⏱   **cook: 25 mins** ⏱

There is a delicious surprise of creamy herb and garlic soft cheese hidden inside these tender chicken parcels!

INGREDIENTS

4 chicken breasts, skin removed

100 g/3½ oz full fat soft cheese,
flavoured with herbs and garlic

8 slices Parma ham

150 ml/5 fl oz red wine

150 ml/5 fl oz Chicken Stock
(see page 13)

1 tbsp brown sugar

NUTRITIONAL INFORMATION	
Calories 272	
Protein 29g	
Carbohydrate 4g	
Sugars 4g	
Fat 13g	
Saturates 6g	

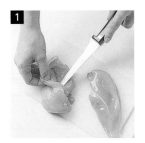

variation

Try adding 2 finely chopped sun-dried tomatoes to the soft cheese in step 2, if you prefer.

1 Using a sharp knife, make a horizontal slit along the length of each chicken breast to form a wide pocket.

2 Beat the cheese with a wooden spoon to soften it. Spoon the cheese into the pockets of the chicken breasts. Wrap 2 slices of Parma ham around each chicken breast and secure firmly in place with a length of string.

3 Pour the wine and Chicken Stock into a large frying pan and bring to the boil. When the mixture is just starting to boil, add the sugar and stir to dissolve.

4 Add the chicken breasts to the mixture in the frying pan. Leave to simmer for 12–15 minutes, or until the chicken is tender and the juices run clear when a skewer is inserted into the thickest part of the meat. Remove the chicken from the pan with a slotted spoon, set aside and keep warm.

5 Reheat the sauce and boil until reduced and thickened. Remove the string from the chicken and cut into slices. Pour the sauce over the chicken to serve.

chicken cacciatora

⏲ **cook: 1 hour**   ⏱ **prep: 20 mins**   **serves 4**

This is a popular Italian classic in which browned chicken quarters are cooked in a tomato and pepper sauce.

NUTRITIONAL INFORMATION	
Calories	.397
Protein	.37g
Carbohydrate	.22g
Sugars	.4g
Fat	.17g
Saturates	.4g

INGREDIENTS

1 roasting chicken, about 1.5 kg/

3 lb 5 oz, cut into 6 or 8 serving pieces

125 g/4½ oz plain flour

salt and pepper

3 tbsp olive oil

150 ml/5 fl oz dry white wine

1 green pepper, deseeded and sliced

1 red pepper, deseeded and sliced

1 carrot, finely chopped

1 celery stick, finely chopped

1 garlic clove, crushed

200 g/7 oz canned chopped tomatoes

variation

This dish is even more warm and flavoursome if you add an extra clove of crushed garlic.

1 Rinse the chicken pieces and pat dry with kitchen paper. Place the flour on a plate, season well with salt and pepper and mix. Lightly dust the chicken pieces with the seasoned flour.

2 Heat the oil in a large frying pan. Add the chicken and cook over a medium heat for 3–4 minutes,

until browned all over. Remove from the pan with a slotted spoon and set aside.

3 Drain off all but 2 tablespoons of the fat in the pan. Add the wine and stir for a few minutes, then add the peppers, carrot, celery and garlic, season with salt and pepper to taste and simmer for 15 minutes.

4 Add the chopped tomatoes to the pan. Cover and simmer for 30 minutes, stirring often, until the chicken is completely cooked through. Check the seasoning before serving piping hot.

butterflied poussins

serves 4   **prep: 15 mins**   **cook: 12 mins**

*The perfect alternative to roast chicken when you find
yourself short of time or just fancy a change, these little
birds are simply split open and grilled until tender.*

INGREDIENTS

4 poussins

55 g/2 oz butter

1 tbsp lemon juice

1 tbsp chopped fresh parsley,

plus extra to garnish

1 tsp chopped fresh tarragon

salt and pepper

mixed salad leaves, to serve

NUTRITIONAL INFORMATION	
Calories 470	
Protein 39g	
Carbohydrate 0g	
Sugars 0g	
Fat 35g	
Saturates 15g	

variation

Omit the herbs and stir 1 tablespoon
mustard powder, 1 tablespoon paprika
and 1 tablespoon Worcestershire sauce
into the melted butter for a spicy dish.

cook's tip

You can thread the skewers
crossways through the
poussins, if you like. Push a
skewer through a wing and
out through the thigh on the
opposite side. Repeat with the
other skewer on the other side.

1 Preheat the grill to high.
If the poussins are
trussed, remove and discard
the string. Using poultry shears
or kitchen scissors, cut along
either side of the backbone of
each bird and remove. Lay the
poussins down and flatten
gently with a rolling pin or the
heel of your hand. Thread a

long skewer from wing to wing
and from leg to leg through
each bird to keep them flat.

2 Melt the butter, brush
it over the poussins and
reserve the remainder. Place
the poussins on a grill rack,
skin side uppermost. Sprinkle
with lemon juice, parsley and
tarragon and season to taste
with salt and pepper.

3 Cook under the
preheated grill for
6 minutes, or until golden.
Turn them over, brush with the
remaining melted butter and
grill for a further 6 minutes,
or until cooked through.
Remove the skewers and
transfer to warmed serving
plates. Garnish with extra
parsley and serve immediately
with mixed salad leaves.

fish & shellfish

Fish is the busy cook's best friend – versatile, tasty, healthy and quick to cook. Nutritionists recommend that we should eat fish at least twice a week and this superb collection of delicious and speedy recipes is just what the doctor ordered. Dishes range from familiar favourites and classic dishes, such as Trout with Almonds (see page 176), Sole Meunière (see page 183) and Thai Prawn Curry (see page 202), to more unusual and contemporary recipes, such as Blackened Fish (see page 174), Monkfish in a Ruby Grapefruit Sauce (see page 179) and Catalan Mussels (see page 208). There are tasty midweek suppers, such as Finnan Haddie (see page 177) and Mediterranean Cod (see page 184), and sophisticated dinner-party dishes, such as Lobster Thermidor (see page 193) and Grilled Scallops & Prawns with Citrus Butter (see page 191). Your guests will never believe that you 'just threw it together in a few minutes after work'.

Inspiration comes from across the world, with recipes from places as far apart as France, the United States, Pakistan, Italy, Scotland, Thailand and Mexico, and all kinds of fish and shellfish are featured, from cod to red snapper and from scallops to salmon. Whatever your tastes, from fiery hot Balti Prawns (see page 203) to satisfying Haddock in a Cheese Jacket (see page 173), and from the elegant simplicity of Salmon with Watercress Cream (see page 180) to tasty baked Crab Creole (see page 197), you can be sure that the world is your oyster.

haddock in a cheese jacket

cook: 12–15 mins   **prep: 15 mins**   **serves 4**

NUTRITIONAL INFORMATION

Calories 386

Protein 43g

Carbohydrate 7g

Sugars 1g

Fat 21g

Saturates 10g

variation

You could use any white fish fillets, such as cod, coley, whiting or hake, if you prefer.

Rather than a cheese sauce, these fish fillets are smothered in a more unusual cheese-flavoured paste that gives them a lovely golden jacket, making them especially popular with children.

INGREDIENTS

2 tbsp olive oil, plus extra for brushing

4 haddock fillets, about 175 g/6 oz each

grated rind and juice of 2 lemons

salt and pepper

115 g/4 oz Gruyère cheese, grated

4 tbsp fresh white breadcrumbs

4 tbsp crème fraîche

4 garlic cloves, finely chopped

TO GARNISH

lemon wedges

fresh parsley sprigs

cook's tip

It is quite easy to overcook fish. When the fish is done, the flesh should be opaque nearly all the way through and it should flake easily when tested with a fork.

1 Preheat the oven to 200°C/400°F/Gas Mark 6. Brush a roasting tin or large ovenproof dish with olive oil and arrange the fish in it in a single layer. Sprinkle with a little lemon juice and season to taste with salt and pepper.

2 Mix the olive oil, cheese, breadcrumbs, crème fraîche, garlic, lemon rind and 6 tablespoons of the remaining lemon juice together in a large bowl and season to taste with salt and pepper. Spread the cheese paste evenly over the fish fillets.

3 Bake in the oven for 12–15 minutes, or until the fish is cooked through. Transfer to warmed serving plates, garnish with lemon wedges and parsley sprigs and serve immediately.

blackened fish

serves 4   **prep: 10 mins**   **cook: 6–8 mins**

Contrary to popular opinion, this fashionable Cajun dish is not in the least bit traditional – in fact, it was first created at the end of the twentieth century.

INGREDIENTS

1 tsp black peppercorns

1 tsp fennel seeds

1 tsp cayenne pepper

1 tsp dried oregano

1 tsp dried thyme

3 garlic cloves, finely chopped

2 tbsp polenta

4 monkfish fillets, about
175 g/6 oz each, skinned

3 tbsp corn oil

TO GARNISH

thinly pared strips of lime rind

lime halves

NUTRITIONAL INFORMATION

Calories 225

Protein 29g

Carbohydrate 7g

Sugars 0g

Fat 10g

Saturates 1g

variation

Use this spice mixture for blackened chicken. Coat 4 skinless, boneless chicken breasts, about 175 g/6 oz each. Fry for 3 minutes on each side.

cook's tip

If you would like a spicier flavour, then rub the Cajun spice mix into the flesh of the fish and leave to stand for 10–15 minutes. Proceed from Step 3 in main recipe.

1 Crush the peppercorns lightly in a mortar with a pestle. Mix the peppercorns, fennel seeds, cayenne, oregano, thyme, garlic and polenta in a shallow dish.

2 Place the monkfish, 1 fillet at a time, in the spice mixture and press gently to coat all over. Shake off any excess.

3 Heat the corn oil in a large, heavy-based frying pan. Add the monkfish and cook for 3–4 minutes on each side, or until tender and cooked through. Serve garnished with the lime rind and lime halves.

trout with almonds

serves 2 **prep: 5 mins** ⏲ **cook: 15–20 mins** ⏲

The simple elegance and delicate flavour of this classic combination ensures its continuing popularity. Serve with new potatoes and freshly cooked broccoli for a delicious meal at any time.

INGREDIENTS

40 g/1½ oz plain flour

salt and pepper

2 trout, about 350 g/12 oz
each, cleaned

55 g/2 oz butter

25 g/1 oz flaked almonds

2 tbsp dry white wine

NUTRITIONAL INFORMATION

Calories	700
Protein	. . . . .59g
Carbohydrate	. . . . .17g
Sugars	. . . . .1g
Fat	. . . . .44g
Saturates	. . . . .19g

1 Spread the flour out on a large, flat plate and season to taste with salt and pepper. Coat the trout in the seasoned flour, shaking off any excess.

2 Melt half the butter in a large, heavy-based frying pan. Add the fish and cook over a medium heat for 6–7 minutes on each side, or until tender and cooked through. Transfer the trout to warmed plates with a fish slice, cover and keep warm.

3 Melt the remaining butter in the frying pan. Add the almonds and cook, stirring frequently, for 2 minutes, or until golden brown. Add the wine, bring to the boil and boil for 1 minute. Spoon the almonds and sauce over the trout and serve immediately.

variation

Substitute either rainbow trout or salmon for the trout, if you prefer.

finnan haddie

cook: 20 mins　　　　**prep: 5 mins**　　　　serves 4

Finnan haddock is, in fact, a small whole haddock that has been soaked in brine before cold smoking. However, you can use undyed smoked haddock fillet for this traditional Scottish dish.

NUTRITIONAL INFORMATION

Calories 320

Protein 33g

Carbohydrate 4g

Sugars 4g

Fat 19g

Saturates 10g

INGREDIENTS

500 g/1 lb 2 oz smoked haddock, skinned and cut into chunks

225 ml/8 fl oz milk

125 ml/4 fl oz single cream

25 g/1 oz unsalted butter

pepper

4 eggs

cook's tip

Look for undyed, smoked haddock, which is a more attractive colour, has a better flavour and is healthier. It is usually available from most supermarkets.

1 Preheat the oven to 180°C/350°F/Gas Mark 4. Place the chunks of fish in a large ovenproof dish. Pour the milk and cream into a small saucepan, add the butter, season to taste with pepper and heat gently until the butter has melted. Pour the mixture over the fish.

2 Bake in the preheated oven for 20 minutes, or until the fish is tender.

3 Meanwhile, bring a small saucepan of water to the boil. Break an egg into a cup, stir the water to create a small 'whirlpool' and slide in the egg. Poach for

3–4 minutes, or until the white is set, but the yolk is still soft. Remove and drain, trimming any stray strings of white, if necessary. Poach the remaining eggs in the same way. Top the fish with the eggs and serve.

monkfish in a ruby grapefruit sauce

cook: 15 mins   **prep: 10 mins**   serves 4

NUTRITIONAL INFORMATION

Calories	380
Protein	33g
Carbohydrate	11g
Sugars	11g
Fat	23g
Saturates	13g

Monkfish fillets are always a good choice for a fish dish because there are no irritating little pin bones hidden inside and the delicious flesh has a firm, meaty texture.

INGREDIENTS

25 g/1 oz butter	juice of 2 ruby grapefruit
800 g/1 lb 12 oz monkfish fillets, cut into chunks	4 tbsp double cream
	100 ml/3½ fl oz fish stock
2 tbsp lemon juice	1 tbsp sunflower oil
salt and pepper	1 ruby grapefruit, cut into segments,
3 carrots, thinly sliced	to garnish

variation

Substitute the fish stock with Chicken Stock (see page 13), if you prefer, and replace the ruby grapefruit with 1 large orange.

1 Melt half the butter in a large, heavy-based frying pan. Sprinkle the fish with the lemon juice, season to taste with salt and pepper, then add to the frying pan and cook over a medium heat for 2½–3 minutes on each side.

2 Meanwhile, melt the remaining butter in a heavy-based saucepan. Add the carrots and cook over a low heat, stirring frequently, for 10 minutes, or until tender. Stir in the grapefruit juice, cream, fish stock and oil and simmer gently for 5 minutes. Remove the saucepan from the heat and leave to cool slightly.

3 Transfer the carrot and grapefruit mixture to a blender or food processor and process until a smooth purée forms. Season to taste with salt and pepper. Spoon the sauce on to 4 warmed plates, top with the monkfish chunks, garnish with the grapefruit segments and serve.

cook's tip

Monkfish is usually sold skinned, but sometimes the transparent grey membrane that surrounds the flesh is still in place. Peel this off before cutting and cooking the fish.

salmon with watercress cream

serves 4 **prep: 5 mins** ⟲ **cook: 20 mins** ⟲

Once a luxurious and expensive treat, salmon is now widely available at an affordable price as a result of fish farming. However, if you have the chance to buy wild salmon, do so, as it has an incomparable flavour and a finer texture.

INGREDIENTS

300 ml/10 fl oz crème fraîche

2 tbsp snipped fresh dill

25 g/1 oz unsalted butter

1 tbsp sunflower oil

4 salmon fillets, about 175 g/6 oz
each, skinned

1 garlic clove, finely chopped

100 ml/3½ fl oz dry white wine

1 bunch of watercress, finely chopped

salt and pepper

variation

If watercress is unavailable, then replace with the same amount of rocket or baby spinach leaves.

cook's tip

Fresh dill goes particularly well with fish, especially salmon, as it has a delicate aniseed flavour. It cannot withstand high temperatures, so is best used at the end of cooking or as a garnish.

1 Pour the crème fraîche into a large, heavy-based saucepan and heat gently to simmering point. Remove the saucepan from the heat, stir in the dill and reserve until required.

2 Melt the butter with the sunflower oil in a heavy-based frying pan. Add the salmon fillets and cook over a medium heat for 4–5 minutes on each side, or until cooked through. Remove the fish from the frying pan, cover and keep warm.

3 Add the garlic to the frying pan and cook, stirring frequently, for 1 minute. Pour in the white wine, bring to the boil and cook until reduced. Stir the crème fraîche mixture into the frying pan and cook for 2–3 minutes, or until thickened.

4 Stir in the watercress and cook until just wilted. Season to taste with salt and pepper. Place the salmon fillets on warmed serving plates, spoon the watercress sauce over them and serve immediately.

sole meunière

cook: 12 mins   **prep: 5 mins**   **serves 4**

Sole has a delicate and subtle flavour, so it is best cooked very simply, rather than being smothered in a rich sauce. This classic French recipe is the best way to do it.

INGREDIENTS

225 ml/8 fl oz milk

115 g/4 oz plain flour

salt and pepper

700 g/1 lb 9 oz Dover sole fillets

25 g/1 oz butter

1–2 tbsp sunflower oil

2 tbsp chopped fresh parsley

lemon wedges, to garnish

variation

A classic variation is Sole aux Légumes Poêles, in which the fish is served with pan-fried vegetables, such as red pepper, cucumber and aubergine.

cook's tip

In spite of their shared name, lemon sole is unrelated to Dover sole. It is rather a shame because it suffers by comparison, yet is a tasty fish in its own right.

1 Pour the milk into a large, shallow dish. Place the flour on a large, flat plate and season to taste with salt and pepper.

2 Dip the sole in the milk and then in the flour, turning to coat. Shake off any excess.

3 Melt the butter with the sunflower oil in a large, heavy-based frying pan. Add the fish fillets, in batches, and cook over a low heat for 2–3 minutes on each side, or until lightly browned. Keep each batch warm while you cook the remaining fish, then sprinkle with the parsley and serve immediately, garnished with the lemon wedges.

mediterranean cod

serves 4   **prep: 10 mins**   **cook: 15 mins**

This is a perfect example of the healthy Mediterranean diet that nutritionists recommend – and what is more, it tastes fabulous. Serve with a fresh, crisp salad for a delicious lunch.

INGREDIENTS

400 g/14 oz canned chopped tomatoes

1 garlic clove, finely chopped

1 tbsp sun-dried tomato paste

1 tbsp Pernod

1 tbsp capers, drained and rinsed

55 g/2 oz black olives, stoned

salt and pepper

4 cod steaks, about 175 g/6 oz each

150 ml/5 fl oz dry white wine

1 bay leaf

¼ tsp black peppercorns

thinly pared strip of lemon rind

fresh flat-leaved parsley sprigs,
to garnish

NUTRITIONAL INFORMATION

Calories	219
Protein	. . . . .33g
Carbohydrate	. . . . .4g
Sugars	. . . . .3g
Fat	. . . . .4g
Saturates	. . . . .1g

cook's tip

Use a vegetable peeler to pare a thin strip of lemon rind from a lemon. The recipe uses fresh flat-leaved parsley rather than curly for the garnish, as it has a more pronounced flavour.

1 Place the chopped tomatoes, garlic, tomato paste, Pernod, capers and olives in a large, heavy-based saucepan and season to taste with salt and pepper. Heat gently, stirring occasionally.

2 Meanwhile, place the cod steaks in a single layer in a large, heavy-based frying pan and pour the wine over them. Add the bay leaf, peppercorns and lemon rind and bring to the boil. Reduce the heat, cover and simmer for 10 minutes, or until the fish is tender.

3 Transfer the cod to a warmed serving dish with a fish slice. Sieve the cooking liquid into the tomato mixture and bring to the boil. Boil for 1–2 minutes, or until slightly reduced and thickened, then spoon the sauce over the fish. Garnish with parsley sprigs and serve immediately.

skate in black butter sauce

🕙 cook: 10–15 mins   🕗 prep: 5 mins   serves 4

The title of this classic recipe is misleading, as the butter does not burn and turn black. In fact, it turns a delicious brown colour, with a flavour that complements the sweet flesh of the skate.

NUTRITIONAL INFORMATION

Calories 229

Protein 21g

Carbohydrate 1g

Sugars 1g

Fat 12g

Saturates 7g

INGREDIENTS

675 g/1 lb 8 oz skate wings

600 ml/1 pint fish stock

225 ml/8 fl oz dry white wine

salt and pepper

55 g/2 oz butter

2 tbsp lemon juice

2 tsp capers, drained and rinsed

2 tbsp chopped fresh parsley

cook's tip

Skate is not at its best when freshly caught, but its flavour improves with keeping for 2–3 days. It may have a smell of ammonia – removed by rinsing and patting dry. If the smell is strong, don't buy it.

1 Place the fish in a large, heavy-based frying pan or flameproof casserole, pour in the fish stock and wine and season to taste with salt and pepper. Bring to the boil, reduce the heat and simmer for 10–15 minutes, or until the fish is tender.

2 Meanwhile, melt the butter in a separate large, heavy-based frying pan and cook over a very low heat until it turns brown, but not black. Stir in the lemon juice, capers and parsley and heat for a further 1–2 minutes.

3 Transfer the skate wings to warmed serving plates with a fish slice, pour the black butter sauce over them and serve.

veracruz red snapper

serves 4　　　**prep: 5 mins, plus** ⏲
30 mins marinating

cook: 25 mins ⏲

One of Mexico's most popular dishes, this looks, smells and tastes absolutely out of this world, and would be a perfect choice as a main course for a dinner party.

INGREDIENTS

4 red snapper fillets	pinch of dried marjoram
salt and pepper	55 g/2 oz green olives, stoned
2 tbsp lime juice	and halved
125 ml/4 fl oz corn oil	2 tbsp capers, drained and rinsed
1 onion, chopped	2 pickled green chillies, drained,
2 garlic cloves, finely chopped	deseeded and sliced
675 g/1 lb 8 oz tomatoes, peeled	55 g/2 oz butter
and chopped	3 slices white bread, crusts removed
1 bay leaf	

NUTRITIONAL INFORMATION

Calories	557
Protein	. . . . .37g
Carbohydrate	. . . . .15g
Sugars	. . . . .7g
Fat	. . . . .39g
Saturates	. . . . .11g

variation

Replace the red snapper with red mullet and, if you prefer, use sunflower or vegetable oil instead of the corn oil.

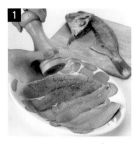

cook's tip

Adding lime or lemon juice to fish helps to make the flesh tender, but don't leave the fish too long in the lime juice, otherwise the juice will begin to cook the fish.

1 Place the red snapper fillets in a large, shallow, non-metallic dish in a single layer and season to taste with salt and pepper. Pour the lime juice over them and leave to marinate until required.

2 Heat the corn oil in a large, heavy-based frying pan. Add the onion and garlic and cook over a low heat, stirring occasionally, for 5 minutes, or until the onion has softened. Add the chopped tomatoes and cook, stirring occasionally, for a further 10 minutes, or until thickened and pulpy. Stir in the bay leaf, dried marjoram, green olives, capers and chillies and add the fish fillets. Cook for 10 minutes, or until the fish is tender.

3 Meanwhile, melt the butter in a separate frying pan. Cut the bread into triangles and fry for 2–3 minutes on each side, or until golden brown. Drain on kitchen paper. Remove and discard the bay leaf from the fish and vegetables. Transfer to a warmed serving dish, garnish with the fried bread and serve.

noodles with chilli & prawns

serves 4   **prep: 10 mins** ⏱   **cook: 5 mins** ⏱

This is a simple dish to prepare and is packed with flavour, making it an ideal, easy-to-make dish for special occasions.

INGREDIENTS

250 g/9 oz thin glass noodles

2 tbsp sunflower oil

1 onion, sliced

2 red chillies, deseeded and very finely chopped

4 lime leaves, thinly shredded

1 tbsp fresh coriander

2 tbsp palm or caster sugar

2 tbsp nam pla (Thai fish sauce)

450 g/1 lb raw tiger prawns, peeled and deveined

NUTRITIONAL INFORMATION

Calories 259

Protein 28g

Carbohydrate 20g

Sugars 9g

Fat 8g

Saturates 1g

variation

You can use ordinary cooked prawns instead of the tiger prawns, if you like. Cook them with the noodles for 1 minute only, to heat through.

cook's tip

Glass noodles, also known as bean thread noodles or cellophane noodles, are made from mung bean starch. They are available from Chinese food shops and large supermarkets.

1 Place the noodles in a large bowl. Pour over enough boiling water to cover and leave to stand for 5 minutes. Drain thoroughly and set aside until required.

2 Place a wok or frying pan over a high heat until warm, then add the sunflower oil and heat until really hot. Add the onion, red chillies and lime leaves to the wok and stir-fry for 1 minute.

3 Add the coriander, sugar, nam pla and prawns to the wok and stir-fry for a further 2 minutes, or until the prawns turn pink.

4 Add the drained noodles to the wok, toss to mix well and stir-fry for 1–2 minutes, or until heated through. Transfer the noodles and prawns to warmed serving bowls and serve immediately.

scallops on skewers

serves 4   **prep: 10 mins** ⏲   **cook: 8 mins** ⏲

Scallops can easily be overcooked, when they become unpleasantly tough. However, they are an ideal choice for the busy cook with little time. This simple dish, which can be cooked under the grill or on a barbecue, will serve four people as a main course or eight as a starter.

INGREDIENTS

48 prepared scallops, thawed if frozen

juice of 1 lemon

24 slices of prosciutto

olive oil, for brushing

mixed salad leaves

pepper

lemon wedges, to garnish

NUTRITIONAL INFORMATION

Calories	.498
Protein	.80g
Carbohydrate	.8g
Sugars	.0g
Fat	.16g
Saturates	.5g

cook's tip

The corals, or roe, are not used in this dish. It is an interesting cultural difference that the corals are prized in Europe but not eaten in the United States.

1 Preheat the grill to medium. Sprinkle the scallops with the lemon juice. Cut the prosciutto into strips, then wrap a strip around each scallop and thread them on to presoaked wooden skewers, 3–4 at a time.

2 Brush the scallops with olive oil and place them on a large baking sheet. Cook under the preheated grill for 4 minutes on each side, or until the scallops are opaque and tender.

3 Make a bed of mixed salad leaves on individual serving plates and divide the skewers between them. Season to taste with pepper, garnish with lemon wedges and serve.

grilled scallops & prawns with citrus butter

cook: 8–9 mins   **prep: 10 mins**   **serves 4**

Seafood and citrus fruit have a natural affinity with each other and this dish will taste equally delicious whether you use limes or lemons to flavour the butter. Unpeeled prawns look attractive, but you can peel them, if you like.

NUTRITIONAL INFORMATION

Calories	.337
Protein	.25g
Carbohydrate	.9g
Sugars	.4g
Fat	.23g
Saturates	.13g

INGREDIENTS

12 prepared scallops, thawed if frozen

12 raw tiger prawns

finely grated rind and juice of 1 lime
or lemon

1 egg yolk

6 tbsp melted butter

1 tbsp snipped fresh dill or chopped
fresh chervil

salt and pepper

2 red onions, cut into wedges

olive oil, for brushing

cook's tip

If using wooden skewers, soak them in warm water for 30 minutes, drain, pat dry, then thread the food on to them. Soaking prevents the skewers burning under the grill or on the barbecue.

1 Preheat the grill to medium. Place the scallops and prawns in a large, shallow, non-metallic dish, add half the citrus rind and half the juice and toss well.

2 Beat the egg yolk with the remaining citrus rind and juice in a small bowl. Gradually whisk in the melted butter, 1 tablespoon at a time.

Continue to whisk until the mixture is thick and smooth. Stir in the dill and season to taste with salt and pepper.

3 Brush the onion wedges with olive oil and cook under the preheated grill for 5 minutes, turning them once. Meanwhile, thread the scallops and prawns on to presoaked wooden skewers, place them

under the grill and cook for 1½–2 minutes on each side, or until the scallops become opaque and the prawns have changed colour.

4 Remove the seafood from the skewers and place on a warmed serving plate. Surround them with the onion wedges, pour the citrus butter over them and serve.

lobster thermidor

cook: 15 mins   **prep: 15 mins**   **serves 4**

NUTRITIONAL INFORMATION	
Calories 570	
Protein 38g	
Carbohydrate 10g	
Sugars 5g	
Fat 34g	
Saturates 19g	

A little extravagant, but this is the perfect dish for an extra special occasion and is guaranteed to impress.

INGREDIENTS

2 cooked lobsters,	2 tsp Dijon mustard
about 750 g/1 lb 10 oz each	salt and pepper
55 g/2 oz butter	6 tbsp dry white wine
1 shallot, chopped	3 tbsp double cream
25 g/1 oz plain flour	4 tbsp freshly grated Parmesan cheese
300 ml/10 fl oz milk	
1½ tsp chopped fresh chervil	TO GARNISH
1 tsp chopped fresh tarragon	lemon slices
1½ tsp chopped fresh parsley	fresh parsley sprigs

variation

Lobster Newburg has a richer sauce, as it is made with double cream and egg yolk. Use Madeira instead of wine and ¼ teaspoon cayenne instead of herbs.

cook's tip

You can polish the half-shells of the lobster with a few drops of olive oil to make the dish look even more attractive, if you like.

1 Preheat the grill to medium. Twist off and discard the lobster heads and pull off the claws. Crack the claws with a small hammer and remove the flesh. Using a sharp knife, split the lobsters in half lengthways and remove and discard the intestinal vein. Remove the flesh and reserve. Scrub the half-shells under cold running water and drain

upside down on kitchen paper. Cut the lobster flesh into 2-cm/¾-inch thick slices.

2 Melt the butter in a heavy-based saucepan. Add the shallot and cook over a low heat for 4–5 minutes, or until softened. Sprinkle in the flour and cook, stirring constantly, for 2 minutes. Remove the saucepan from the

heat and gradually stir in the milk. Return the saucepan to the heat and bring to the boil, stirring. Cook, stirring, until thickened and smooth.

3 Reduce the heat, stir in the herbs and mustard and season to taste with salt and pepper. Remove the saucepan from the heat and whisk in the wine and cream.

Return to a low heat and simmer until thickened. Add the lobster flesh and heat through for 2–3 minutes.

4 Divide the mixture between the half-shells and sprinkle with the Parmesan cheese. Cook under the hot grill until the topping is golden and bubbling. Serve, garnished with lemon slices and parsley.

prawns in anchovy sauce

serves 4   **prep: 10 mins** ☾   **cook: 15 mins** ⏱

Finger bowls and napkins are essential for eating these tasty prawns as they require peeling. The dish makes a perfect starter as well as a light supper. Serve with plenty of fresh crusty bread to help mop up all the delicious juices.

INGREDIENTS

6 tbsp olive oil

4 garlic cloves, finely chopped

5 canned anchovy fillets, drained and chopped

3 tbsp finely chopped fresh flat-leaved parsley

6 tbsp dry white wine

400 g/14 oz canned chopped tomatoes

pinch of chilli powder

salt and pepper

1.5 kg/3 lb 5 oz large raw prawns, unpeeled

TO GARNISH

lemon wedges

fresh flat-leaved parsley sprigs

NUTRITIONAL INFORMATION	
Calories	.347
Protein	.35g
Carbohydrate	.4g
Sugars	.3g
Fat	.20g
Saturates	.3g

variation

Replace the lemon wedges with lime wedges and use chopped, peeled and deseeded fresh tomatoes instead of canned, if you prefer.

cook's tip

When buying prawns, always choose ones that look and smell fresh, and that have shiny shells. Tiger prawns are the best choice for this dish.

1 Heat the olive oil in a large, heavy-based saucepan. Add the garlic, anchovies and parsley and cook, stirring frequently, for 5 minutes. Add the wine and cook, stirring constantly, until reduced.

2 Add the tomatoes with their can juices and the chilli powder and season to taste with salt and pepper. Add the prawns, reduce the heat and simmer gently for 10 minutes, or until the prawns have changed colour.

3 Divide the prawns and sauce between warmed serving dishes, garnish with lemon wedges and parsley sprigs and serve immediately.

gamberi fritti

serves 4 | **prep: 5 mins** | **cook: 10 mins**

Like most Italian dishes, the keynotes of these delicately-flavoured prawns are simplicity and the best-quality fresh ingredients.

INGREDIENTS

4 tbsp olive oil

32 large raw prawns, unpeeled

3 garlic cloves, finely chopped

125 ml/4 fl oz dry white vermouth

3 tbsp passata

salt and pepper

3 tbsp chopped fresh

flat-leaved parsley

NUTRITIONAL INFORMATION

Calories 209

Protein 15g

Carbohydrate 3g

Sugars 2g

Fat 12g

Saturates 2g

cook's tip

Prawns are cooked as soon as they turn pink. Large, unpeeled prawns may take slightly longer to cook. To test if they are done, cut a prawn in half and if the flesh is opaque, then they are cooked.

1 Heat the olive oil in a large, heavy-based saucepan. Add the prawns and cook over a high heat, stirring and tossing constantly, until they change colour.

2 Add the garlic and vermouth and cook, stirring and tossing the prawns constantly, until the liquid comes to the boil.

3 Add the passata and season to taste with salt and pepper. Stir the prawns until they are thoroughly coated. Transfer to warmed serving plates, sprinkle with the chopped parsley and serve immediately.

crab creole

⏱ **cook: 20 mins**   ⏱ **prep: 10 mins**   **serves 6**

You can use fresh, frozen and thawed, or canned crabmeat for this recipe. You could also substitute the sherry with dry white wine.

NUTRITIONAL INFORMATION	
Calories	349
Protein	18g
Carbohydrate	5g
Sugars	1g
Fat	28g
Saturates	15g

INGREDIENTS

3 hard-boiled eggs, shelled

1 tsp Dijon mustard

85 g/3 oz butter

¼ tsp cayenne pepper

3 tbsp dry sherry

1 tbsp snipped fresh dill

400 g/14 oz crabmeat

125 ml/4 fl oz double cream

3 spring onions, thinly sliced

salt and pepper

55 g/2 oz dried white breadcrumbs

cook's tip

For perfect boiled eggs, bring the eggs to room temperature, then bring a pan of water to the boil. Reduce the heat and cook the eggs for 12 minutes. Plunge in cold water and leave for 8 minutes before shelling.

1 Preheat the oven to 180°C/350°F/Gas Mark 4. Separate the hard-boiled egg whites and yolks. Place the yolks in a bowl and mash lightly with a fork. Add the mustard, 55 g/2 oz of the butter and the cayenne pepper and mash to a paste. Stir in the sherry and dill.

2 Flake the crabmeat into a separate bowl, removing any pieces of shell or cartilage. Chop the egg whites and stir them into the crabmeat with the cream and spring onions. Season to taste with salt and pepper.

3 Divide the mixture between 6 individual ovenproof dishes. Sprinkle with the breadcrumbs and dot with the remaining butter. Bake in the preheated oven for 20 minutes, or until the topping is golden brown. Serve immediately.

fillets of red mullet & pasta

serves 4　　　　**prep: 15 mins** ⟳　　　　**cook: 1 hour** ⟳

A simple mixture of garlic, herbs, lemon, nutmeg and anchovies perfectly complements the sweet, delicate flesh of red mullet.

INGREDIENTS

1 kg/2 lb 4 oz red mullet fillets

300 ml/10 fl oz dry white wine

4 shallots, finely chopped

1 garlic clove, crushed

3 tbsp finely chopped mixed fresh herbs

finely grated rind and juice of 1 lemon

pinch of freshly grated nutmeg

3 anchovy fillets, roughly chopped

salt and pepper

2 tbsp double cream

1 tsp cornflour

450 g/1 lb dried vermicelli

1 tbsp olive oil

TO GARNISH

1 fresh mint sprig

lemon slices

lemon rind

NUTRITIONAL INFORMATION

Calories 457

Protein 39g

Carbohydrate 44g

Sugars 3g

Fat 12g

Saturates 5g

variation

You can substitute red snapper for the red mullet, if you like, and if you like garlic, add a small extra clove, crushed.

cook's tip

Remember to protect your hands when you transfer the casserole from the oven to the hob – the handles will be hot – and be careful not to burn your kitchen work surface by resting the hot dish on it.

1 Preheat the oven to 180°C/350°F/Gas Mark 4. Put the red mullet fillets in a large casserole. Pour over the wine and add the shallots, garlic, herbs, lemon rind and juice, nutmeg and anchovies. Season to taste, then cover and bake in the preheated oven for 35 minutes.

2 Transfer the mullet to a warmed dish with a wooden spoon. Set aside and keep warm.

3 Place the casserole on the hob over a high heat and bring the cooking liquid to the boil. Reduce the heat and simmer

for 25 minutes, until reduced by half. Mix the cream and cornflour and stir into the sauce to thicken.

4 Meanwhile, bring a saucepan of lightly salted water to the boil. Add the vermicelli and oil and cook for 8–10 minutes, until tender

but still firm to the bite. Drain the pasta and transfer to a warmed serving dish.

5 Arrange the red mullet fillets on top of the vermicelli and pour over the sauce. Garnish with a fresh mint sprig, slices of lemon and strips of lemon rind and serve.

trout with smoked bacon

serves 4   **prep: 35 mins** ᗷ   **cook: 25 mins** ⏱

Most trout available nowadays is farmed rainbow trout, however, if you can, buy wild brown trout for this recipe.

INGREDIENTS

15 g/½ oz butter, for greasing

4 trout, about 275 g/9½ oz each, gutted and cleaned

salt and pepper

12 anchovies in oil, drained and chopped

2 apples, peeled, cored and sliced

4 fresh mint sprigs

juice of 1 lemon

12 slices rindless smoked fatty bacon

450 g/1 lb dried tagliatelle

1 tbsp olive oil

TO GARNISH

2 apples, cored and sliced

4 fresh mint sprigs

NUTRITIONAL INFORMATION

Calories 802

Protein 68g

Carbohydrate 54g

Sugars 8g

Fat 36g

Saturates 10g

variation

Replace the mint sprigs with another fresh herb of your choice, if you like. Parsley also works well in this recipe.

cook's tip

Use eating apples such as Cox's or Braeburn apples for this dish. Place the apple slices in cold water mixed with a little lemon juice to prevent them from browning while you prepare the rest of the recipe.

1 Preheat the oven to 200°C/400°F/Gas Mark 6. Grease a deep baking tray with the butter.

2 Open up the cavities of each trout and rinse with warm salt water. Season each cavity with salt and pepper. Divide the anchovies, sliced apples and mint sprigs between each of the cavities. Sprinkle the lemon juice into each cavity.

3 Carefully wrap the body of each trout, except the head and tail, with three slices of smoked bacon wound in a spiral. Arrange the trout on the prepared baking tray with the loose ends of bacon tucked underneath. Season with pepper and bake in the preheated oven for 20 minutes, turning the trout over after 10 minutes.

4 Meanwhile, bring a large saucepan of lightly salted water to the boil. Add the tagliatelle and olive oil and cook for 12 minutes, until tender but still firm to the bite. Drain the pasta and transfer to a large, warmed serving dish.

5 Remove the trout from the oven and arrange on the tagliatelle. Garnish with sliced apples and fresh mint sprigs and serve immediately.

thai prawn curry

serves 4   **prep: 10 mins**   **cook: 10 mins**

Tiger prawns are cooked in a fragrant mixture of green curry paste, herbs and coconut milk to produce a delicious meal in minutes.

INGREDIENTS

2 tbsp groundnut oil

2 tbsp Thai green curry paste

4 kaffir lime leaves, shredded

1 lemon grass stalk, crushed and finely chopped

450 g/1 lb raw tiger prawns, peeled and deveined

225 ml/8 fl oz coconut milk

2 tbsp nam pla (Thai fish sauce)

½ cucumber, deseeded and cut into thin batons

12 fresh basil leaves

4 fresh green chillies, deseeded and sliced

NUTRITIONAL INFORMATION

Calories	.216
Protein	.27g
Carbohydrate	.5g
Sugars	.3g
Fat	.10g
Saturates	.2g

cook's tip

Lemon grass stalks, available in Asian food shops and some supermarkets, are used widely in South-east Asia. To prepare a stalk, remove and discard the outer layer, crush with a rolling pin and chop or slice.

1 Heat the groundnut oil in a preheated wok or large, heavy-based frying pan. Add the curry paste and cook, stirring frequently, until it gives off its aroma and is beginning to bubble. Add the lime leaves, lemon grass and prawns and stir-fry for 2 minutes, or until the prawns are beginning to change colour.

2 Pour in the coconut milk, stir gently, then bring the mixture to the boil. Reduce the heat and simmer, stirring occasionally, for 5 minutes, or until the prawns are tender.

3 Stir in the Thai fish sauce, cucumber batons, basil leaves and sliced chillies. Transfer to warmed serving dishes and serve immediately.

balti prawns

cook: 10 mins   **prep: 10 mins**   **serves 4**

*This curry is not for the faint-hearted, as it is fiery hot. Serve with
naan bread and a cooling cucumber raita to soothe the taste buds.*

NUTRITIONAL INFORMATION	
Calories	180
Protein	16g
Carbohydrate	8g
Sugars	6g
Fat	10g
Saturates	1g

INGREDIENTS

4 fresh green chillies

2 onions, roughly chopped

2 tbsp lemon juice

2 tbsp tomato purée

3 tbsp chopped fresh coriander

1 tsp ground coriander

1 tsp chilli powder

½ tsp ground turmeric

pinch of salt

1 tbsp water (optional)

3 tbsp sunflower oil

32 large raw prawns, peeled
and deveined

cook's tip

For a cucumber raita, beat
300 ml/10 fl oz natural
yogurt, then stir in ¼ diced
cucumber, 1 chopped fresh
chilli, ¼ teaspoon ground
cumin and salt to taste.
Chill before serving.

1 Deseed and thinly slice
2 of the chillies and
reserve for the garnish. Place
the whole chillies, onions,
lemon juice, tomato purée,
2 tablespoons of the fresh
coriander, the ground
coriander, chilli powder,
turmeric and salt in a food
processor and process until
a smooth paste forms. If
necessary, thin with the water.

2 Heat the sunflower oil
in a preheated wok or
large, heavy-based frying pan.
Add the spice paste and
cook, stirring constantly, for
4 minutes, or until thickened.

3 Add the prawns and
cook, stirring constantly,
for 4–5 minutes, or until they
have changed colour. Transfer
to a warmed serving plate,
garnish with the sliced chillies
and remaining fresh coriander
and serve immediately.

prawn pasta bake

serves 4   **prep: 10 mins**   **cook: 50 mins**

This recipe is ideal for a substantial supper. You can use whatever pasta you like, but the tricolour varieties will give colourful results, and make the dish look especially tempting.

INGREDIENTS

225 g/8 oz tricolour pasta shapes	425 ml/15 fl oz skimmed milk
1 tbsp vegetable oil	salt and pepper
175 g/6 oz button mushrooms, sliced	4 medium tomatoes, sliced thinly
1 bunch spring onions, trimmed and chopped	25 g/1 oz fresh breadcrumbs
	25 g/1 oz reduced-fat Cheddar cheese, grated
400 g/14 oz canned tuna in brine, drained and flaked	
175 g/6 oz cooked, peeled prawns, thawed if frozen	TO SERVE
2 tbsp cornflour	wholemeal bread
	fresh salad

variation

You can stir 2 tablespoons of chopped fresh parsley into the pasta mixture in Step 3, if you like. Sprinkle the surface with parsley rather than spring onions.

cook's tip

Cornflour is usually mixed into a smooth paste with a little liquid before being added to the remaining liquid. This prevents the sauce from turning lumpy.

1 Preheat the oven to 190°C/375°F/Gas Mark 5. Bring a large saucepan of water to the boil and cook the pasta according to the instructions on the packet. Drain well.

2 Meanwhile, heat the vegetable oil in a frying pan and cook the mushrooms and all but a handful of the spring onions for 4–5 minutes, until softened.

3 Place the cooked pasta in a bowl and mix in the spring onions, mushrooms, tuna and prawns.

4 Blend the cornflour with a little of the milk to make a paste. Pour the remaining milk into a saucepan and stir in the paste. Heat, stirring, until the sauce begins to thicken. Season well. Add the sauce to the pasta mixture and mix well. Transfer to an ovenproof gratin dish and place on a baking tray.

5 Arrange the tomato slices over the pasta and sprinkle with the breadcrumbs and cheese.

Bake in the preheated oven for 25–30 minutes, until golden. Serve sprinkled with the reserved spring onions and accompanied with wholemeal bread and salad.

indian cod with tomatoes

serves 4   prep: 5 mins   cook: 25 mins

Quick and easy – cod steaks are cooked in a rich tomato and coconut sauce to produce tender, succulent results.

INGREDIENTS

3 tbsp vegetable oil

4 cod steaks, about 2.5 cm/1 inch thick

salt and pepper

1 onion, finely chopped

2 garlic cloves, crushed

1 red pepper, deseeded and chopped

1 tsp ground coriander

1 tsp ground cumin

1 tsp ground turmeric

½ tsp garam masala

400 g/14 oz canned chopped tomatoes

150 ml/5 fl oz coconut milk

1–2 tbsp chopped fresh coriander or parsley

variation

The mixture may be flavoured with a tablespoonful of curry powder or curry paste instead of the mixture of spices in Step 2, if you wish.

cook's tip

The heat must be kept low in Step 2 to prevent the spices from burning and losing their flavour. Frequent stirring will help to prevent them sticking to the bottom of the pan.

1 Heat the oil in a frying pan, add the fish steaks, season with salt and pepper and cook for 2–3 minutes, until browned on both sides but not cooked through. Remove from the pan and reserve.

2 Add the onion, garlic, red pepper and spices and cook over a very low heat for 2 minutes, stirring frequently. Add the tomatoes, bring to the boil and simmer for 5 minutes.

3 Add the fish steaks to the pan and simmer gently for 8 minutes, or until the fish is cooked through. Remove from the pan with a slotted spoon and keep warm on a serving dish.

4 Add the coconut milk and coriander to the pan and reheat gently. Spoon the sauce over the cod steaks and serve immediately.

catalan mussels

serves 4   **prep: 15 mins** ⏲   **cook: 15 mins** ⏱

Mussels are cooked in a piquant tomato sauce with just a hint of spice. You can serve them hot, lukewarm in the Spanish style, or cold. Provide plenty of crusty bread or rolls to mop up the juices.

INGREDIENTS

2 kg/4 lb 8 oz live mussels, scrubbed
and debearded
5 tbsp olive oil
2 onions, chopped
2 garlic cloves, finely chopped
4 large tomatoes, peeled, deseeded
and finely chopped
1 bay leaf
1 tbsp brandy
½ tsp paprika
salt and pepper
crusty bread, to serve

NUTRITIONAL INFORMATION

Calories	315
Protein	. . . . .28g
Carbohydrate	. . . . .11g
Sugars	. . . . .9g
Fat	. . . . .17g
Saturates	. . . . .3g

cook's tip

When buying mussels, choose ones that have a fresh, salty smell and undamaged shells. Do not pick any mussels that are heavy, as they may be full of sand, or any that feel very light, as they may be dead.

1 Discard any mussels with broken or damaged shells and any that do not shut immediately when sharply tapped with the back of a knife.

2 Heat the oil in a large, heavy-based saucepan or flameproof casserole. Add the onion and garlic and cook over a low heat, stirring occasionally, for 5 minutes, or until softened. Add the tomatoes and bay leaf and cook, stirring occasionally, for a further 5 minutes.

3 Stir in the brandy and paprika and season to taste with salt and pepper. Increase the heat, add the mussels, cover the saucepan and cook, shaking the saucepan occasionally, for 5 minutes, or until the shells have opened. Discard the bay leaf and any mussels that have not opened. Transfer the mussels to a warmed serving dish and pour the sauce over them. Serve immediately with crusty bread or leave to cool.

thai fragrant mussels

🕐 cook: 5 mins   🕐 prep: 10 mins   serves 4

Lemon grass, galangal and lime leaves delicately flavour and perfume this simple and elegant Eastern dish. Serve with a sweet chilli sauce for dipping, if you like.

NUTRITIONAL INFORMATION

Calories 133

Protein 26g

Carbohydrate 1g

Sugars 0g

Fat 3g

Saturates 1g

INGREDIENTS

2 kg/4 lb 8 oz live mussels, scrubbed
and debearded

2 lemon grass stalks, lightly crushed

5-cm/2-inch piece of galangal or
fresh root ginger, bruised

5 kaffir lime leaves, shredded

3 garlic cloves

300 ml/10 fl oz water

salt

cook's tip

Galangal is used extensively in South-east Asia. It is a member of the ginger family, but is spicier than fresh root ginger. It can be found in Asian food shops. If it is unavailable, then use fresh root ginger instead.

1 Discard any mussels with broken or damaged shells and any that do not shut immediately when sharply tapped with the back of a knife.

2 Place the mussels, lemon grass, galangal, lime leaves, garlic and water into a large, heavy-based saucepan or flameproof casserole and season to taste with salt. Bring to the boil, then cover and cook over a high heat, shaking the saucepan occasionally, for 5 minutes, or until the shells have opened.

3 Remove and discard the flavourings and any mussels that have not opened. Divide the mussels between 4 soup bowls with a slotted spoon. Tilt the pan and allow any sand to settle, then spoon the cooking liquid over the mussels and serve immediately.

desserts

If the proof of the pudding is in the eating, then this is the chapter for you.
While those great stand-bys, fresh fruit and pots of yogurt, certainly have a place in the
busy cook's life, they can become tedious if served every night, and a home-made dessert
makes a welcome change. At a family meal or a dinner party, dessert is the final, triumphant
flourish and the great thing is that the range of hot and cold dishes that can be prepared
at speed is surprisingly extensive. Bakes, fritters, creams, cheesecakes and even light-as-air
soufflés can be made in minutes and need no special skills or expertise.

There are tantalizing treats for the sweet-toothed, such as Almost Instant Toffee Pudding (see
page 245) and Fried Bananas in Maple Syrup (see page 248); popular children's choices, such as
Apple Fritters (see page 229) and Strawberry Baked Alaska (see page 241); and rich and creamy
dishes for more sophisticated palates, such as Zabaglione (see page 234) and Lemon Posset (see
page 242). Many of the recipes, while still taking only a short time in the kitchen, can be
prepared in advance and so are ideal for entertaining. Cold desserts usually benefit from being
chilled, even for just 30 minutes, but this doesn't have to cause delays. Because you can make
them so quickly, do so before you begin to prepare the main course – they can then chill
in the refrigerator while you are cooking and eating your meal.

sugar-topped fruit cake

serves 10   **prep: 15 mins**   **cook: 1 hour**

Soft apple purée and whole blackberries make this fruit cake delicious, and a sugar-cube topping adds crunch and sweetness.

INGREDIENTS

15 g/½ oz butter, for greasing

350 g/12 oz cooking apples

3 tbsp lemon juice

300 g/10½ oz wholemeal self-raising flour

½ tsp baking powder

1 tsp ground cinnamon, plus extra for dusting

175 g/6 oz prepared blackberries, thawed if frozen, plus extra to decorate

175 g/6 oz light muscovado sugar

1 medium egg, beaten

200 ml/7 fl oz low-fat natural fromage frais

55 g/2 oz white or brown sugar cubes, lightly crushed

sliced eating apple, to decorate

NUTRITIONAL INFORMATION

Calories 227

Protein 5g

Carbohydrate 53g

Sugars 30g

Fat 1g

Saturates 0.2g

variation

Try replacing the blackberries with blueberries. You can use the canned or frozen variety if fresh blueberries are not available.

cook's tip

Make sure that the apples are completely soft before beating them, to ensure a smooth texture in the finished cake.

1 Preheat the oven to 190°C/375°F/Gas Mark 5. Grease a 900-g/2-lb loaf tin with the butter and line with baking paper. Core, peel and finely dice the apples. Place them in a saucepan with the lemon juice, bring to the boil, cover and simmer for 10 minutes until soft and pulpy. Beat well and set aside to cool.

2 Sift the flour, baking powder and cinnamon into a bowl, adding any husks that remain in the sieve. Stir in 115 g/4 oz of the blackberries and the sugar.

3 Make a well in the centre of the ingredients and add the egg, fromage frais and cooled apple purée. Mix well to incorporate thoroughly. Spoon the mixture into the prepared loaf tin and smooth over the top.

4 Sprinkle with the remaining blackberries, pressing them down into the cake mixture, and top with the crushed sugar lumps. Bake for 40–45 minutes. Leave to cool in the tin.

5 Remove the cake from the tin and peel away the lining paper. Serve dusted with cinnamon and decorated with extra blackberries and apple slices.

raspberry fusilli

serves 4   **prep: 5 mins** (ᐱ)   **cook: 20 mins** (ᐱ)

This is the ultimate in complete self-indulgence – a truly delicious dessert that tastes every bit as good as it looks.

INGREDIENTS

175 g/6 oz dried fusilli

700 g/1 lb 9 oz raspberries

2 tbsp caster sugar

1 tbsp lemon juice

4 tbsp flaked almonds

3 tbsp raspberry liqueur

NUTRITIONAL INFORMATION	
Calories 235	
Protein 7g	
Carbohydrate 36g	
Sugars 20g	
Fat 7g	
Saturates 1g	

variation

You could use any sweet berry for this dessert. Try strawberries or blackberries and use the correspondingly flavoured fruit liqueur.

1 Bring a large saucepan of lightly salted water to the boil. Add the fusilli and cook for 8–10 minutes, until tender but still firm to the bite. Drain the fusilli thoroughly, return to the saucepan and set aside to cool.

2 Using a spoon, firmly press 225 g/8 oz of the raspberries through a sieve set over a mixing bowl to form a smooth purée. Put the purée in a small saucepan with the sugar and simmer over a low heat, stirring occasionally, for 5 minutes. Stir in the lemon juice and set the sauce aside until required.

3 Add the remaining raspberries to the fusilli in the saucepan and mix together well. Transfer the raspberry and fusilli mixture to a serving dish.

4 Preheat the grill to medium. Spread the almonds out on a baking tray and toast under the grill for 1–2 minutes, until golden brown. Remove and set aside to cool slightly.

5 Stir the raspberry liqueur into the reserved raspberry sauce and mix well until very smooth. Pour the sauce over the fusilli, sprinkle over the toasted almonds and serve.

quick tiramisu

cook: 0 mins   **prep: 15 mins**   **serves 4**

This quick version of one of the most widely-loved, traditional Italian desserts takes just minutes to make.

NUTRITIONAL INFORMATION

Calories	387
Protein	................9g
Carbohydrate	.........22g
Sugars	...............17g
Fat	..................28g
Saturates	.............15g

INGREDIENTS

225 g/8 oz mascarpone or
full-fat soft cheese
1 egg, separated
2 tbsp natural yogurt
2 tbsp caster sugar
2 tbsp dark rum
2 tbsp strong black coffee
8 sponge fingers
2 tbsp grated dark chocolate

cook's tip

Mascarpone is an Italian soft cream cheese made from cow's milk. It has a rich, silky smooth texture and a deliciously creamy flavour. It can be eaten as it is with fresh fruits or flavoured with coffee or chocolate.

1 Put the cheese in a large bowl, add the egg yolk and yogurt and beat until smooth.

2 Whisk the egg white until stiff but not dry, then whisk in the sugar and carefully fold into the cheese mixture. Divide half of the mixture between 4 sundae glasses.

3 Mix the rum and coffee together in a shallow dish. Dip the sponge fingers into the rum mixture, break them in half, or into smaller pieces if necessary, and divide between the glasses.

4 Stir any remaining coffee mixture into the remaining cheese mixture and divide between the glasses.

5 Sprinkle with the grated chocolate. Serve immediately, or chill in the refrigerator until required.

carrot & ginger cake

serves 10   **prep: 15 mins** 🕐   **cook: 1 hr 15 mins** ⏲

This melt-in-the-mouth version of a favourite cake has a fraction of the fat of the traditional cake, and is packed with vitamins.

INGREDIENTS

15 g/½ oz butter, for greasing	3 tbsp corn oil
225 g/8 oz plain flour	juice of 1 medium orange
1 tsp baking powder	
1 tsp bicarbonate of soda	**FROSTING**
2 tsp ground ginger	225 g/8 oz low-fat soft cheese
½ tsp salt	4 tbsp icing sugar
175 g/6 oz light muscovado sugar	1 tsp vanilla essence
225 g/8 oz carrots, grated	
2 pieces stem ginger in syrup, drained and chopped	**TO DECORATE**
25 g/1 oz fresh root ginger, grated	grated carrot
55 g/2 oz seedless raisins	stem ginger
2 medium eggs, beaten	ground ginger

NUTRITIONAL INFORMATION

Calories	.249
Protein	.7g
Carbohydrate	.46g
Sugars	.28g
Fat	.6g
Saturates	.1g

variation

You could sprinkle the frosting with ground cinnamon instead of ground ginger if you prefer.

cook's tip

Using a loose-bottomed cake tin will make it easier to turn out the cake, but be careful to line the tin well, with no gaps around the edges.

1 Preheat the oven to 180°C/350°F/Gas Mark 4. Grease a 20.5-cm/8-inch round cake tin with the butter and line with baking paper.

2 Sift the flour, baking powder, bicarbonate of soda, ground ginger and salt into a bowl. Stir in the sugar, carrots, stem ginger, fresh root ginger and raisins. Beat the eggs, oil and orange juice together, then pour slowly into the cake mixture. Mix together well.

3 Spoon the mixture into the tin and bake in the oven for 1–1¼ hours, until firm to the touch and a skewer inserted into the centre of the cake comes out clean.

4 To make the frosting, place the soft cheese in a bowl and beat to soften. Sift in the icing sugar and add the vanilla essence. Mix well.

5 Remove the cake from the tin and smooth the frosting over the top. Decorate the cake with grated carrot and ginger and serve.

tuscan puddings

serves 4　　　　　　**prep: 20 mins** ⏱　　　　　　**cook: 15 mins** ♨

These mini baked ricotta puddings are delicious served warm or chilled and will keep in the refrigerator for 3–4 days.

INGREDIENTS

15 g/½ oz butter, for greasing

75 g/2¾ oz mixed dried fruit

250 g/9 oz ricotta cheese

3 egg yolks

50 g/1¾ oz caster sugar

1 tsp cinnamon

finely grated rind of 1 orange,

plus extra to decorate

crème fraîche, to serve (optional)

NUTRITIONAL INFORMATION

Calories	.293
Protein	.9g
Carbohydrate	.28g
Sugars	.28g
Fat	.17g
Saturates	.9g

cook's tip

Crème fraîche has a slightly sour, nutty taste and is very thick. It has the same fat content as double cream. It can be made by stirring cultured buttermilk into double cream and refrigerating overnight.

1 Preheat the oven to 180°C/350°F/Gas Mark 4. Lightly grease 4 mini pudding basins or ramekin dishes with the butter.

2 Put the dried fruit in a bowl and cover with warm water. Leave to soak for 10 minutes.

3 Beat the ricotta cheese with the egg yolks in a bowl. Stir in the caster sugar, cinnamon and orange rind and mix to combine.

4 Drain the dried fruit in a sieve set over a bowl. Mix the drained fruit with the ricotta cheese mixture. Spoon the mixture into the basins or ramekin dishes and bake in the preheated oven for 15 minutes. The tops of the puddings should be firm to the touch but not brown.

5 Turn out the puddings and decorate them with grated orange rind. Serve warm or chilled with a dollop of crème fraîche, if you like.

honey & nut nests

cook: 1 hour   **prep: 10 mins**   **serves 4**

Pistachio nuts and honey are combined with crisp, cooked angel-hair pasta in this unusual and attractive dessert.

NUTRITIONAL INFORMATION	
Calories	.802
Protein	.13g
Carbohydrate	.85g
Sugars	.53g
Fat	.48g
Saturates	.16g

INGREDIENTS

salt

225 g/8 oz angel-hair pasta

115 g/4 oz butter

175 g/6 oz shelled pistachio
nuts, chopped

115 g/4 oz sugar

115 g/4 oz clear honey

150 ml/5 fl oz water

2 tsp lemon juice

Greek-style yogurt, to serve

cook's tip

Angel hair pasta is also known as *capelli d'angelo*. It is long and very fine, and is usually sold in small bunches that already resemble nests.

1 Preheat the oven to 180°C/350°F/Gas Mark 4. Bring a large saucepan of lightly salted water to the boil. Add the angel hair pasta and cook for 8–10 minutes, or until tender but still firm to the bite. Drain the pasta and return to the saucepan. Add the butter and toss to coat the pasta thoroughly. Set aside to cool.

2 Arrange 4 small flan or poaching rings on a baking tray. Divide the angel hair pasta into 8 equal quantities and spoon 4 of them into the rings. Press down lightly. Top the pasta with half of the nuts, then add the remaining pasta. Bake the nests in a preheated oven for 45 minutes, or until golden brown.

3 Meanwhile, put the sugar, honey and water in a saucepan and bring to the boil over a low heat, stirring constantly until the sugar has dissolved completely. Simmer for 10 minutes, add the lemon juice and simmer for a further 5 minutes.

4 Using a palette knife, carefully transfer the cooked angel hair nests to a serving dish. Pour over the honey syrup, sprinkle over the remaining nuts and set aside to cool completely before serving. Serve the Greek-style yogurt separately.

banana & lime cake

serves 10   **prep: 35 mins** ⟳   **cook: 45 mins** ⏱

This substantial cake is ideal served with a mid-afternoon cup of tea. The mashed bananas help to keep the cake moist, and the lime icing gives it extra zing and zest.

INGREDIENTS

15 g/½ oz butter, for greasing

300 g/10½ oz plain flour

1 tsp salt

1½ tsp baking powder

175 g/6 oz light muscovado sugar

1 tsp grated lime rind

1 medium egg, beaten

1 medium banana, mashed with 1 tbsp lime juice

150 ml/5 fl oz low-fat natural fromage frais

115 g/4 oz sultanas

TOPPING

115 g/4 oz icing sugar

1–2 tsp lime juice

½ tsp finely grated lime rind

TO DECORATE

banana chips

finely grated lime rind

NUTRITIONAL INFORMATION

Calories	.235
Protein	.5g
Carbohydrate	.55g
Sugars	.31g
Fat	.1g
Saturates	.0.3g

variation

For a delicious alternative, replace the lime rind and juice with orange and the sultanas with chopped apricots.

cook's tip

Banana chips are dried slices of banana, and can be found in the baking section of supermarkets, or in health food shops.

1 Preheat the oven to 180°C/350°F/Gas Mark 4. Grease a deep 18-cm/7-inch round cake tin with the butter and line with baking paper.

2 Sift the flour, salt and baking powder into a mixing bowl and stir in the sugar and lime rind. Make a well in the centre of the dry ingredients and add the egg, banana, fromage frais and sultanas. Mix well until thoroughly incorporated.

3 Spoon the mixture into the prepared tin and smooth the surface. Bake in the preheated oven for 40–45 minutes, until firm to the touch or until a skewer inserted into the centre comes out clean. Leave to cool for 10 minutes, then turn out on to a wire rack.

4 To make the topping, sift the icing sugar into a small bowl and mix with the lime juice to form a soft, but not too runny, icing. Stir in the grated lime rind. Drizzle the icing over the cake, letting it run down the sides.

5 Decorate the cake with banana chips and lime rind. Let the cake stand for 15 minutes so that the icing sets.

indian mango dessert

serves 4   **prep: 10 mins** ⏱   **cook: 0 mins** ⏱

Perhaps because the main course often tends to be spicy, Indian cooks will often serve a sweet, refreshing and creamy dessert as a contrast at the end of a meal.

INGREDIENTS

2 ripe mangoes

300 ml/10 fl oz double cream, plus
extra to decorate

2 tsp caster sugar

NUTRITIONAL INFORMATION

Calories 412

Protein 2g

Carbohydrate 15g

Sugars 15g

Fat 39g

Saturates 24g

variation

Use other exotic fruits. Cut 400 g/14 oz guavas in half, sprinkle with lime juice and scoop out the flesh. Don't use kiwi fruit as it curdles the cream.

1 Place a mango on a chopping board, narrow-side down, and cut a thick slice lengthways as close to the stone as possible. Turn the mango round and slice the other side as close to the stone as possible. Cut off any flesh remaining on the stone. Reserve a few unpeeled, thin mango slices for the decoration. Without cutting through the skin of the mango halves, score the flesh in the 2 thick slices in criss-cross lines about 1 cm/½ inch apart. Fold the halves inside out and slice off the cubes of flesh. Repeat with the second mango.

2 Place the mango flesh in a blender or food processor and process until a smooth purée forms.

3 Beat the cream with the sugar until stiff, then gently fold in the mango purée. Spoon into glass dishes, cover and leave to chill in the refrigerator until required. Serve decorated with extra whipped cream and the reserved mango slices.

somerset pears

⏱ **cook: 20 mins**   ⏲ **prep: 5 mins**   **serves 4**

The pears must be ripe but still quite firm for this dish. Choose a variety such as Williams, Conference or Beth. Serve with vanilla ice cream or cream to create the perfect finale to a dinner party.

NUTRITIONAL INFORMATION	
Calories	.139
Protein	.1g
Carbohydrate	.32g
Sugars	.32g
Fat	.0g
Saturates	.0g

INGREDIENTS

225 ml/8 fl oz medium sweet cider

55 g/2 oz caster sugar

thinly pared rind and juice of 1 lemon

pinch of freshly grated nutmeg

4 pears

1 Pour the cider into a large, heavy-based saucepan and add the sugar, lemon rind, lemon juice and nutmeg. Heat gently, stirring constantly, until the sugar has dissolved.

2 Peel the pears using a swivel-blade vegetable peeler, but leave the stalks intact. Add them to the saucepan and poach gently, turning frequently, for 15 minutes.

3 Transfer the pears to warmed bowls with a slotted spoon. Increase the heat under the saucepan and stir the cooking liquid occasionally, until slightly reduced and syrupy. Spoon over the pears and serve.

variation

Pears are also delicious if they are poached gently in the same amount of red wine, caster sugar and a pinch of cloves.

florentines

serves 10　　　**prep: 20 mins** ⏱　　　**cook: 15 mins** ⏱

These luxury biscuits will be popular at any time of the year, but make a particularly wonderful treat at Christmas.

INGREDIENTS

50 g/1¾ oz butter

50 g/1¾ oz caster sugar

25 g/1 oz plain flour, sieved

50 g/1¾ oz almonds, chopped

50 g/1¾ oz chopped mixed peel

25 g/1 oz raisins, chopped

25 g/1 oz glacé cherries, chopped

finely grated rind of ½ lemon

125 g/4½ oz dark chocolate, melted

NUTRITIONAL INFORMATION

Calories 186

Protein 2g

Carbohydrate 22g

Sugars 19g

Fat 11g

Saturates 5g

variation

Replace the dark chocolate with white chocolate or, for a dramatic effect, cover half of the florentines in dark chocolate and half in white.

cook's tip

To melt the chocolate, break into pieces and place in a heatproof bowl over a saucepan of gently simmering water and stir until smooth.

1 Preheat the oven to 180°C/350°F/Gas Mark 4. Line 2 large baking trays with baking paper.

2 Heat the butter and caster sugar in a small saucepan until the butter has just melted and the sugar has dissolved. Remove the saucepan from the heat.

3 Stir in the flour and mix well. Stir in the chopped almonds, mixed peel, raisins, cherries and lemon rind. Place teaspoonfuls of the mixture well apart on the prepared baking trays and bake in the preheated oven for 10 minutes, or until lightly golden.

4 As soon as the florentines are removed from the oven, press the edges into neat shapes while still on the baking trays, using a biscuit cutter. Leave to cool on the baking trays until firm, then transfer to a wire rack to cool completely.

5 Spread the melted chocolate over the smooth side of each florentine. As the chocolate begins to set, mark wavy lines in it with a fork. Leave the florentines until set, chocolate-side up.

char-cooked pineapple

serves 4   **prep: 10 mins**   **cook: 10 mins**

Fresh pineapple slices are brushed with a buttery fresh ginger and brown sugar baste and cooked on the barbecue.

INGREDIENTS

1 fresh pineapple

GINGER BUTTER

125 g/4½ oz butter
85 g/3 oz light muscovado sugar
1 tsp finely grated fresh root ginger

TOPPING

225 g/8 oz natural fromage frais
½ tsp ground cinnamon
1 tbsp light muscovado sugar

NUTRITIONAL INFORMATION

Calories	.461
Protein	.5g
Carbohydrate	.45g
Sugars	.44g
Fat	.30g
Saturates	.20g

variation

If you prefer, substitute ½ teaspoon ground ginger for the fresh ginger. Light muscovado sugar gives the best flavour, but you can also use soft brown sugar.

1 Prepare the fresh pineapple by cutting off the spiky top. Peel the pineapple with a sharp knife, remove the 'eyes' and cut the flesh into thick slices.

2 To make the ginger butter, put the butter, sugar and ginger into a small saucepan and heat gently until melted. Transfer to a heatproof bowl and keep warm at the side of the barbecue, ready for basting the fruit.

3 To make the topping, mix the fromage frais, cinnamon and sugar together in a bowl. Cover and chill in the refrigerator until ready to serve.

4 Brush the pineapple slices well with the ginger butter baste, then barbecue for 2 minutes on each side.

5 Serve the char-cooked pineapple with a little extra ginger butter poured over. Top with a spoonful of the spiced fromage frais.

italian chocolate truffles

cook: 5 mins   **prep: 5 mins**   **makes 24**

These truffles, flavoured with almonds and chocolate, are simplicity itself to make. Served with coffee, they are the perfect end to a meal.

NUTRITIONAL INFORMATION

Calories	82
Protein	. . . . .1g
Carbohydrate	. . . . .8g
Sugars	. . . . .7g
Fat	. . . . .5g
Saturates	. . . . .3g

INGREDIENTS

175 g/6 oz dark chocolate

2 tbsp almond-flavoured or orange-flavoured liqueur

40 g/1½ oz unsalted butter

50 g/1¾ oz icing sugar

50 g/1¾ oz ground almonds

50 g/1¾ oz grated milk chocolate

variation

If you prefer, you can roll the truffles in grated white chocolate to give them a contrasting coating.

1 Melt the dark chocolate with the liqueur in a heatproof bowl set over a saucepan of simmering water, stirring until well combined.

2 Add the butter and stir until it has melted. Stir in the icing sugar and the ground almonds. Leave the mixture in a cool place until firm, then roll into 24 balls.

3 Place the grated chocolate on a plate and roll the truffles in the chocolate to coat them. Place the truffles in paper sweet cases and chill in the refrigerator until required.

apple fritters

⏲ **cook: 8–10 mins**   ⏱ **prep: 10 mins**   **serves 4**

NUTRITIONAL INFORMATION

Calories 240

Protein 4g

Carbohydrate 37g

Sugars 26g

Fat 10g

Saturates 2g

variation

Replace the apple with 1 small
pineapple, peeled and cut into rings.
Banana fritters would also be delicious.
Use 4 bananas instead of apples.

*Succulent apple rings, enclosed in crispy batter and sprinkled with
cinnamon sugar, are sure to become firm family favourites.*

INGREDIENTS

sunflower oil, for deep-frying	55 g/2 oz plain flour
1 large egg	2 tsp ground cinnamon
pinch of salt	55 g/2 oz caster sugar
175 ml/6 fl oz water	4 eating apples, peeled and cored

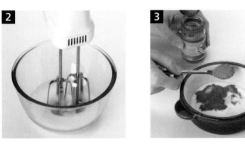

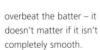

cook's tip

The best and easiest way to
core an apple is to use an
apple corer. Push the corer into
the stalk end of the apple and
twist to cut around the core,
then pull it out and discard.

1 Pour the sunflower oil
into a deep fryer or
large, heavy-based saucepan
and heat to 180–190°C/
350–375°F, or until a cube of
bread browns in 30 seconds.

2 Meanwhile, using an
electric mixer, beat the
egg and salt together until
frothy, then quickly whisk in
the water and flour. Do not
overbeat the batter – it
doesn't matter if it isn't
completely smooth.

3 Mix the cinnamon and
sugar together in a
shallow dish and reserve.

4 Slice the apples into
5-mm/¼-inch thick
rings. Spear with a fork, 1 slice
at a time, and dip in the batter
to coat. Add to the hot oil, in
batches, and cook for 1 minute
on each side, or until golden
and puffed up. Remove with
a slotted spoon and drain on
kitchen paper. Keep warm
while you cook the remaining
batches. Transfer to a large
serving plate, sprinkle with the
cinnamon sugar and serve.

vanilla ice cream

serves 6   **prep: 5 mins** ⏱   **cook: 15 mins** ⏱

This home-made version of real vanilla ice cream is absolutely delicious and so easy to make. A tutti-frutti variation is also provided.

INGREDIENTS

600 ml/1 pint double cream

1 vanilla pod

pared rind of 1 lemon

4 eggs, beaten, and 2 egg yolks

175 g/6 oz caster sugar

NUTRITIONAL INFORMATION

Calories 626

Protein 7g

Carbohydrate 33g

Sugars 33g

Fat 53g

Saturates 31g

variation

For tutti-frutti ice cream, follow the same method, omitting the vanilla pod, and stir in 100 g/3½ oz dried fruit soaked in sherry just before freezing.

1 Place the cream in a heavy-based saucepan over a low heat and warm gently, whisking. Add the vanilla pod, lemon rind, eggs and egg yolks to the saucepan, increase the heat and stir until the mixture reaches just below boiling point.

2 Reduce the heat to low and cook for 8–10 minutes, whisking the mixture continuously, until thickened. Stir in the sugar, then set aside to cool.

3 Strain the cooled cream mixture through a sieve. Slit open the vanilla pod, scoop out the tiny black seeds and stir them into the cream.

4 Pour the mixture into a shallow freezer container with a lid and freeze overnight, until set. Scoop out to serve.

peaches & mascarpone

 cook: 10 mins   prep: 10 mins   serves 4

If you prepare these in advance, all you have to do is pop the peaches on the barbecue when you are ready to serve them.

NUTRITIONAL INFORMATION

Calories 301

Protein 6g

Carbohydrate 24g

Sugars 24g

Fat 20g

Saturates 9g

INGREDIENTS

4 peaches

175 g/6 oz mascarpone cheese

40 g/1½ oz pecan nuts or

walnuts, chopped

1 tsp sunflower oil

4 tbsp maple syrup

1 Cut the peaches in half and remove the stones. If you are preparing this recipe in advance, press the peach halves together again and wrap in clingfilm until required.

2 Mix the mascarpone and nuts together in a bowl until well combined.

Leave to chill in the refrigerator until required.

3 To serve, brush the peaches with a little oil and place on a rack set over medium hot coals. Barbecue for 5–10 minutes, turning once, until hot.

4 Transfer the peaches to a serving dish and top with the mascarpone mixture. Drizzle the maple syrup over the top and serve at once.

variation

You can use nectarines instead of peaches for this recipe. Remember to choose ripe but firm fruit which will keep its shape when barbecued.

pineapple bake

serves 6   **prep: 15 mins**   **cook: 10 mins**

*A tropical taste of warm, fresh pineapple and a light-as-air
rum-flavoured topping will bring a smile to everyone's face.*

INGREDIENTS

1 pineapple	1 tbsp cornflour
4 tbsp sultanas	½ tsp vanilla essence
2 tbsp raisins	¼ tsp ground ginger
4 tbsp maple syrup	2 egg whites
4 tbsp white rum, such as Bacardi	2 tbsp muscovado sugar
1 egg yolk	

NUTRITIONAL INFORMATION

Calories	.240
Protein	.3g
Carbohydrate	.53g
Sugars	.47g
Fat	.1g
Saturates	.0g

variation

Replace the vanilla essence with
vanilla extract, which is made from
crushed vanilla pods.

cook's tip

There are two important points
to note: make sure that you
buy genuine maple syrup (not
maple-flavoured syrup) and
pure vanilla essence (rather
than artificial, which is made
from clove oil).

1 Preheat the oven to
240°C/475°F/Gas
Mark 9. Using a sharp knife,
cut off the leafy pineapple top
and a 2.5-cm/1-inch slice from
the base and discard. Stand
the pineapple upright on a
large chopping board and slice
off the skin in strips. Use the
point of the knife to remove
any 'eyes' and slice the
pineapple in half lengthways.

Cut out the core, then
slice each pineapple half
horizontally into slices.

2 Arrange the pineapple
slices in a large
ovenproof dish and sprinkle
the sultanas and raisins over
them. Drizzle with half the
maple syrup and half the
rum. Bake in the preheated
oven for 5 minutes.

3 Meanwhile, mix the
remaining maple syrup
and rum, egg yolk, cornflour,
vanilla and ginger together in
a bowl. Whisk the egg whites
in a separate, spotlessly clean,
greasefree bowl until soft
peaks form. Stir 2 tablespoons
of the egg whites into the
egg yolk mixture, then fold
all the egg yolk mixture into
the whites.

4 Spread the topping over
the hot pineapple, sift
the sugar over the top and
return to the oven for
5 minutes, or until golden
brown. Serve immediately.

zabaglione

serves 6   **prep: 5 mins** ⏲   **cook: 5 mins** ⏲

This rich, creamy, Italian dessert must be served as soon as it is ready, but fortunately it takes only moments to prepare.

INGREDIENTS

4 egg yolks

70 g/2½ oz caster sugar

125 ml/4 fl oz Marsala wine

NUTRITIONAL INFORMATION

Calories	115
Protein	2g
Carbohydrate	14g
Sugars	14g
Fat	4g
Saturates	1g

variation

Marsala is the usual wine used in this classic dessert, but other wines and spirits can be used, such as sherry or rum. Serve with amaretti biscuits, if you like.

1 Using an electric mixer, beat the egg yolks with the sugar in a heatproof bowl until pale and creamy.

2 Set the bowl over a saucepan of barely simmering water. Make sure that the base of the bowl does not touch the surface of the water, or the yolks will scramble. Gradually beat in the Marsala and continue beating until the zabaglione is thick, creamy, and has increased in volume.

3 Divide the zabaglione between 6 wine glasses and serve immediately.

grilled peaches & cream

cook: 4 mins   **prep: 10 mins**   **serves 4**

Grilled fruit makes a great dessert, not just because it is quick and easy, but also because it tastes and looks so delicious.

NUTRITIONAL INFORMATION	
Calories	280
Protein	4g
Carbohydrate	35g
Sugars	35g
Fat	15g
Saturates	9g

INGREDIENTS

4 large peaches

2 tbsp brown sugar

½ tsp ground cinnamon

300 ml/10 fl oz soured cream

4 tbsp caster sugar

cook's tip

To stone peaches, cut vertically around the fruit, then twist each half in opposite directions to reveal the stone. Using the point of a knife, prise the stone out, remove it with your fingers and discard.

1 Preheat the grill to medium. Blanch the peaches in boiling water for 1 minute. Refresh under cold running water, then peel, halve, stone and slice. Arrange the slices in 4 individual flameproof dishes.

2 Mix the brown sugar and cinnamon together and sprinkle the mixture over the peaches. Spoon the soured cream on top, then sprinkle 1 tablespoon of caster sugar over each dish.

3 Cook under the preheated grill for 2–3 minutes, or until the caster sugar has melted and caramelized. Serve immediately or leave to cool.

grilled fruit kebabs

cook: 10 mins

prep: 10 mins, plus 10 mins marinating

serves 4

NUTRITIONAL INFORMATION

Calories 176

Protein 2g

Carbohydrate 30g

Sugars 27g

Fat 6g

Saturates 1g

variation

You can use other types of fruit for these kebabs, such as seedless grapes, mango slices and papaya chunks.

Use your time economically when you prepare these kebabs. Mix the marinade, then drop the pieces of fruit into it as you prepare them. Preheat the grill while the fruit is marinating in the luscious mixture of hazelnut oil, lime juice and honey.

INGREDIENTS

2 tbsp hazelnut oil

2 tbsp clear honey

juice and finely grated rind of 1 lime

2 pineapple rings, halved

8 strawberries

1 pear, peeled, cored and thickly sliced

1 banana, peeled and thickly sliced

2 kiwi fruit, peeled and quartered

1 star fruit, cut into 4 slices

cook's tip

Honeys vary widely in flavour and the best quality, with a distinctive taste, is usually made from a single type of blossom. For this recipe, try orange blossom, acacia or lime flower.

1 Preheat the grill to medium. Mix the hazelnut oil, honey, lime juice and rind together in a large, shallow, non-metallic dish. Add the fruit and turn to coat. Leave to marinate for 10 minutes.

2 Thread the fruit alternately on to 4 long metal skewers, beginning with a piece of pineapple and ending with a slice of star fruit.

3 Brush the kebabs with the marinade and cook under the preheated hot grill, brushing frequently with the marinade, for 5 minutes. Turn the kebabs over, brush with the marinade again and grill for a further 5 minutes. Serve immediately.

fruit parcels

serves 4   **prep: 15 mins**   **cook: 10 mins**

Children in particular enjoy this fun way of serving food and you can use virtually any of their favourite fruits. Use orange juice for young diners and orange liqueur for adults.

INGREDIENTS

unsalted butter, for greasing	2 tbsp caster sugar
2 apples	2 tbsp orange liqueur or orange juice
2 bananas	2 tbsp flaked almonds
2 oranges	

NUTRITIONAL INFORMATION

Calories	.206
Protein	.3g
Carbohydrate	.35g
Sugars	.34g
Fat	.6g
Saturates	.2g

variation

Use other fruits, including hulled strawberries, slices of melon, mango and papaya, mandarin segments and pear chunks, if you prefer.

cook's tip

Be careful when opening up the parcels after cooking as they will be extremely hot. It is best if the parcels are left to cool slightly before serving.

1 Preheat the oven to 240°C/475°F/Gas Mark 9. Cut 4 large squares of foil and lightly grease with butter. Quarter and core the apples (but do not peel), then slice. Peel and slice the bananas. Peel the oranges, taking care to remove all the pith, then cut into segments and discard the membranes.

2 Place all the fruit in a large bowl and sprinkle the sugar over it. Add the orange liqueur and sprinkle with the almonds. Mix well.

3 Divide the fruit between the pieces of foil and wrap securely into neat parcels. Place the parcels on a large baking sheet and bake in the preheated oven for 10 minutes. Transfer to serving plates, open up the parcels slightly and serve.

grape brûlée

serves 4 **prep: 5 mins, plus 6 hrs ⏲ chilling (optional)** **cook: 8 mins ⏲**

Although this dessert takes hardly any time to prepare, with only a few minutes needed to caramelize the topping, it is best served chilled. To make the ideal grape brûlée, prepare it at least six hours or up to two days in advance.

INGREDIENTS

225 g/8 oz seedless grapes, halved

225 ml/8 fl oz double cream

2 tbsp brandy

4 tsp caster sugar

4 tbsp demerara sugar

NUTRITIONAL INFORMATION	
Calories	379
Protein	1g
Carbohydrate	31g
Sugars	31g
Fat	27g
Saturates	17g

variation

For a lower-fat version, replace the double cream with natural yogurt and use either red or green grapes.

1 Reserve about 16 of the grape halves for decoration and place the rest in a shallow, flameproof dish.

2 Lightly whip the cream, then beat in the brandy and caster sugar. Spread the cream over the grapes. If there is time, leave to chill in the refrigerator (with the reserved grapes) for at least 6 hours.

3 To serve, preheat the grill to medium. Sprinkle the demerara sugar evenly over the cream and place under the preheated grill for about 8 minutes, or until bubbling and caramelized. Decorate with the reserved grape halves and serve.

strawberry baked alaska

cook: 3–5 mins   **prep: 10 mins**   **serves 6**

This dessert is a first choice for children, and even adults will admit to enjoying the contrast between the cold ice cream and the warm meringue in this perennial favourite. You can use a home-made or store-bought sponge cake for the base.

NUTRITIONAL INFORMATION

Calories 464

Protein 9g

Carbohydrate 63g

Sugars 51g

Fat 21g

Saturates 9g

INGREDIENTS

23-cm/9-inch round sponge cake

2 tbsp sweet sherry or orange juice

5 egg whites

140 g/5 oz caster sugar

600 ml/1 pint strawberry ice cream

175 g/6 oz fresh strawberries, halved, plus whole strawberries, to serve

cook's tip

For the perfect meringue, bring the egg whites to room temperature before whisking. It is worth noting that the fresher the eggs, the greater the volume of the meringue.

1 Preheat the oven to 240°C/475°F/Gas Mark 9. Place the sponge cake in a large, shallow, ovenproof dish and sprinkle with the sherry or orange juice.

2 Whisk the egg whites in a spotlessly clean, greasefree bowl until stiff. Continue to whisk, gradually adding the sugar, until very stiff and glossy.

3 Working quickly, cover the top of the cake with the ice cream and then top with the strawberry halves. Spread the meringue over the cake, making sure that the ice cream is completely covered. Bake in the preheated oven for 3–5 minutes, or until the meringue is golden brown. Serve immediately, with whole strawberries.

lemon posset

serves 4   **prep: 10 mins** 🕒   **cook: 0 mins** 🕒

This is a hugely rich and self-indulgent dessert, but the sharpness of the lemon gives it a wonderfully refreshing flavour.

INGREDIENTS

grated rind and juice of 1 large lemon

4 tbsp dry white wine

55 g/2 oz caster sugar

300 ml/10 fl oz double cream

2 egg whites

lemon slices, to decorate

langues de chat biscuits, to serve

NUTRITIONAL INFORMATION

Calories 408

Protein 3g

Carbohydrate 17g

Sugars 17g

Fat 36g

Saturates 23g

variation

Replace the lemon with the grated rind and juice of 1 orange, decorate with orange slices and serve with amaretti biscuits, if you prefer.

cook's tip

Use only the very freshest eggs for this dish. It is not advisable to serve any dishes containing raw eggs to the very young or old, the infirm, or anyone whose immune system has been compromised.

1 Mix the lemon rind, lemon juice, wine and sugar together in a bowl. Stir until the sugar has dissolved. Add the cream and beat with an electric mixer until soft peaks form.

2 Whisk the egg whites in a separate, spotlessly clean, greasefree bowl until stiff, then carefully fold them into the cream mixture.

3 Spoon the mixture into tall glasses and leave to chill in the refrigerator until required. Serve decorated with lemon slices and accompanied by the biscuits.

almost instant toffee pudding

cook: 15 mins   **prep: 10 mins**   serves 6

NUTRITIONAL INFORMATION

Calories 329

Protein 5g

Carbohydrate 34g

Sugars 24g

Fat 20g

Saturates 12g

variation

Instead of the bread triangles, cut the bread into different shapes, such as fingers or small squares.

This is the ideal dessert for a midweek family supper in autumn or winter, when you have had a busy day and cold weather has sharpened everyone's appetite.

INGREDIENTS

2 eggs	115 g/4 oz unsalted butter
100 ml/3½ fl oz milk	1 tbsp sunflower oil
pinch of ground cinnamon	55 g/2 oz muscovado sugar
6 slices of white bread, crusts removed	4 tbsp golden syrup

cook's tip

Keep the fried bread warm in a medium–hot oven while making the toffee sauce. For a touch of indulgence, serve with some whipped cream.

1 Using a fork, beat the eggs with 6 tablespoons of the milk and the cinnamon in a large, shallow dish. Cut the bread into triangles and place in the dish, in batches if necessary, to soak for 2–3 minutes.

2 Melt half the butter with half the oil in a heavy-based frying pan. Add the bread triangles, in batches, and cook for 2 minutes on each side, or until golden brown, adding a little more butter and oil as necessary Remove with a fish slice, drain on kitchen paper, transfer to serving plates and keep warm.

3 Add the remaining butter and milk to the frying pan with the sugar and golden syrup and cook, stirring constantly, until hot and bubbling. Pour the toffee sauce over the bread triangles and serve.

speedy apricot cheesecake

serves 6 **prep: 15 mins, plus 40 mins chilling** **cook: 2–3 mins**

This delicately flavoured cheesecake needs no baking and is based on basic storecupboard ingredients, although you will need to buy cottage cheese and cream.

INGREDIENTS

425 g/15 oz canned apricot halves in syrup

350 g/12 oz cottage cheese

85 g/3 oz caster sugar

grated rind and juice of 1 lemon

1 tbsp gelatine powder

150 ml/5 fl oz double cream

BASE

55 g/2 oz unsalted butter, plus extra for greasing

115 g/4 oz digestive biscuits, crushed

½ tsp ground cinnamon

TO DECORATE

canned apricots, cut into slices

flaked almonds

variation

Replace the canned apricot halves with other canned fruit, such as peaches, plums or stoned cherries. Alternatively, use fresh fruit, such as strawberries.

cook's tip

Crush the biscuits for the base in a food processor or place them in a large polythene bag and crush with a rolling pin until crumbs form.

1 Grease an 18-cm/7-inch loose-bottomed, round flan tin with butter. To make the base, heat the butter gently in a small saucepan until just melted. Remove from the heat and stir in the biscuit crumbs and cinnamon. Spoon the mixture into the tin and press it evenly all over the base. Chill in the refrigerator while you make the filling.

2 Drain the apricots and reserve the syrup. Place the apricots in a food processor and process until a smooth purée forms. Scrape the purée into a bowl. Rub the cottage cheese through a sieve into the bowl and beat in the sugar, lemon rind and lemon juice until smooth.

3 Place 2 tablespoons of the reserved syrup in a small heatproof bowl and sprinkle the gelatine on the surface. Leave for a few minutes to soften. Set the bowl over a saucepan of barely simmering water and stir until the gelatine has completely dissolved. Leave to cool while you whip the cream until thick. Stir the gelatine syrup into the apricot mixture, then fold in the cream. Spread the filling over the base and leave to chill in the refrigerator until set. Decorate the top with apricot slices and almonds before serving.

fried bananas in maple syrup

serves 4   **prep: 5 mins** ⏲   **cook: 4 mins** ⏲

This almost instant dessert looks good and tastes delicious. For an extra treat, serve it with vanilla ice cream or natural yogurt.

INGREDIENTS

40 g/1½ oz unsalted butter

6 bananas, peeled and diagonally sliced

6 tbsp maple syrup

4 tbsp flaked almonds, to decorate

NUTRITIONAL INFORMATION

Calories	.376
Protein	.4g
Carbohydrate	.61g
Sugars	.55g
Fat	.14g
Saturates	.6g

variation

Substitute the bananas with other fruit, such as pineapple rings or apple slices, if you like.

1 Melt the butter in a large, heavy-based frying pan. Add the bananas and cook over a low heat for 45 seconds on each side.

2 Add the syrup and cook for a further 2 minutes, or until the banana slices have softened.

3 Transfer the bananas to warmed serving dishes, sprinkle with flaked almonds and serve immediately.

veiled country lass

cook: 5 mins | **prep: 10 mins, plus 30 mins chilling (optional)** | **serves 6**

This is a traditional Danish dessert made in layers, so it looks especially attractive in a glass serving dish.

NUTRITIONAL INFORMATION

Calories 539

Protein 4g

Carbohydrate 72g

Sugars 57g

Fat 28g

Saturates 17g

INGREDIENTS

225 g/8 oz rye bread, crusts removed

2 tbsp caster sugar

25 g/1 oz unsalted butter

900 g/2 lb apple purée or apple sauce

225 g/8 oz blackcurrant jam

300 ml/10 fl oz double cream

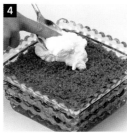

cook's tip

The contrasts in this dessert derive from using rye bread, which has a distinctive flavour and texture, for the crumbs. You could use German black bread, made from a mixture of rye and cornmeal.

1 Tear the bread into pieces, place in a food processor and process until crumbs form. Transfer to a bowl and stir in the sugar.

2 Melt the butter in a large, heavy-based frying pan, add the breadcrumb mixture and cook over a medium heat, stirring occasionally, for 3–5 minutes, or until crisp. Remove the frying pan from the heat and leave to cool slightly.

3 Spoon half the apple purée into the base of a glass serving dish. Cover the purée with half the jam, then spoon on half the breadcrumb mixture. Repeat these layers, ending with the breadcrumb mixture.

4 Using an electric mixer, beat the cream until thickened and stiff, then spread it over the top of the dessert. If you have time, leave to chill for 30 minutes in the refrigerator before serving.

lemon soufflé

cook: 25 mins   **prep: 5 mins**   serves 6

NUTRITIONAL INFORMATION

Calories 177

Protein 7g

Carbohydrate 15g

Sugars 12g

Fat 10g

Saturates 5g

variation

Use the grated rind and juice of
1 orange instead of the lemon,
if you prefer.

*A hot soufflé makes a spectacular end to a meal and this delicious,
lemon-flavoured confection is the perfect palate cleanser. All hot
soufflés will collapse disappointingly if left to stand, so make sure
that you serve it as soon as it is ready.*

INGREDIENTS

25 g/1 oz unsalted butter, plus extra
for greasing

25 g/1 oz icing sugar

300 ml/10 fl oz milk

25 g/1 oz plain flour

grated rind and juice of 1 lemon

5 egg yolks

2 tbsp caster sugar

6 egg whites

cook's tip

If you are planning to serve this
delicious dessert to guests at a
dinner party, you can prepare
the soufflé up to the end of
Step 2 in advance.

1 Preheat the oven to
180°C/350°F/Gas
Mark 4. Grease a 1.4-litre/
2½-pint soufflé dish with
butter and dust the base and
sides with icing sugar. Pour the
milk into a small saucepan and
bring to simmering point.

2 Meanwhile, melt the
butter in a heavy-based
saucepan over a low heat.

Remove from the heat and stir
in the flour until a smooth
paste forms. Gradually stir in
the hot milk. Return to the
heat and cook, stirring, for
2 minutes, or until thickened
and smooth. Stir in the lemon
rind and juice and reserve.

3 Beat the egg yolks with
the caster sugar until
pale, then gradually stir them

into the lemon mixture, adding
only a little at a time.

4 Whisk the egg whites in
a spotlessly clean,
greasefree bowl until stiff
peaks form. Fold the egg
whites into the lemon mixture.
Spoon into the dish and bake
in the preheated oven for
20 minutes, or until risen
and golden brown. Serve.

chocolate fondue

serves 6   **prep: 10 mins** ◔   **cook: 5 mins** ♨

What could be quicker and easier than letting your guests serve themselves? This treat for those with a sweet tooth is traditionally served after a day on the ski slopes.

INGREDIENTS

selection of fresh fruit, such as apples, bananas, pears, seedless grapes, peaches and oranges	225 g/8 oz plain chocolate, broken into pieces
juice of 1 lemon (optional)	6 tbsp double cream
small sponge or Madeira cake	2 tbsp dark rum
	55 g/2 oz icing sugar

NUTRITIONAL INFORMATION	
Calories	.698
Protein	.7g
Carbohydrate	.83g
Sugars	.70g
Fat	.39g
Saturates	.19g

variation

Use white chocolate instead of plain chocolate and use other types of fruit, such as strawberries, grapes, or mango and pineapple chunks.

cook's tip

Make sure that the chocolate is melted over a very low heat. If the chocolate is too hot, then it may burn and turn grainy. Do not let any water splash on to the chocolate, otherwise it will seize and is unusuable.

1 Prepare the fruit according to type, cutting it into bite-sized pieces. Brush apples, pears and bananas with a little lemon juice to prevent them from discolouring. Cut the sponge cake into cubes. Arrange the fruit and cake on several serving plates.

2 Place the chocolate and cream in the top of a double boiler and heat gently, stirring constantly, until melted and smooth. Alternatively, melt the chocolate and cream in a heatproof bowl set over a saucepan of barely simmering water. Remove the saucepan or bowl from the heat.

3 Stir in the rum and sugar. Pour the mixture into a ceramic fondue pot set over a burner and hand the fruit and cake separately. Each guest can then spear their chosen morsel and dip it in the hot chocolate mixture.

A

anchovy sauce 194
antipasto volente 66
apple fritters 229
apricot cheesecake 246
artichoke soup 22
aubergine dipping platter 99

B

bacon with lamb's lettuce 63
baked fennel 95
balti prawns 203
banana & lime cake 220
basic recipes 13
bean & vegetable soup 20
beef
    kebabs 123
    & potato soup 35
    satay 64
    spaghetti & meatballs 146
    steak in orange sauce 126
    stock 13
    stroganoff 122
    tournedos Rossini 125
black butter sauce 185
blackened fish 174
bruschetta 62
butterflied poussins 168

C

Caesar salad 85
Calabrian mushroom soup 18
Caribbean cook-up rice 103
carrots
    & dahl soup 40
    & ginger cake 216
    & orange soup 27
Catalan mussels 208
char-cooked pineapple 226
check list 12
cheese
    aigrettes 109
    fritters 108
    haddock in a jacket 173
    old English soup 26
    sauce 137
    tagliarini with gorgonzola 51
chef's salad 86
chicken
    braised in red wine 163
    butterflied poussins 168
    cacciatore 167

Chinese 158
cordon bleu 156
garlic & herb 166
goujons 97
with green olives 164
honey-glazed 160
& leek soup 38
satay 64
sesame ginger 76
stock 13
tarragon 161
teriyaki 157
Chinese dishes
    chicken 158
    omelette 56
chocolate fondue 252
chunky potato & beef soup 35
citrus butter 191
cod
    Mediterranean 184
    with tomatoes 206
crab
    Creole 197
    partan bree 39
    soup 33
    Thai golden pouches 61
cream of pea soup 24
creamy mushroom sauce 135
crispy seaweed 57
cured meats with olives & tomatoes 72

D

dahl & carrot soup 40
deep-fried seafood 98
dipping platter 99
dressings
    Thousand Island 13
    Vinaigrette 13

E

eggs
    Benedict 114
    Chinese omelette 56
    omelettes with fines herbes 113
    wild mushroom omelettes 112
    zuppa pavese 31
equipment 10–11

F

fajitas 71
fast-food techniques 7
fillets of red mullet & pasta 198

Finnan haddie 177
fish
    antipasto volente 66
    balti prawns 203
    blackened 174
    canned 8
    Catalan mussels 208
    crab Creole 197
    deep-fried seafood 98
    fillets of red mullet & pasta 198
    Finnan haddie 177
    gamberi fritti 196
    haddock in a cheese jacket 173
    Indian cod with tomatoes 206
    lobster thermidor 193
    Mediterranean cod 184
    monkfish in ruby grapefruit sauce 179
    noodles with chilli & prawns 188
    pan-fried scallops & prawns 46
    & potato pâté 92
    prawn pasta bake 204
    prawns in anchovy sauce 194
    salmon with watercress cream 180
    scallops on horseback 46
    scallops on skewers 190
    sesame prawn toasts 54
    skate in black butter sauce 185
    smoked trout with pears 53
    sole meunière 183
    spicy crab soup 33
    Thai fragrant mussels 209
    Thai prawn curry 202
    trout with almonds 176
    trout with smoked bacon 200
    Veracruz red snapper 186
flambéed prawns 50
florentines 224
forward planning 10–11
fresh spaghetti & meatballs 146
fried dishes
    bananas in maple syrup 248
    green tomatoes 117
fritters
    apple 229
    cheese 108
    peanut 119
    spicy sweetcorn 58
fruit parcels 238

G

gamberi fritti 196
gammon in Madeira sauce 136

index

garlic
    croutons 85
    & herb chicken 166
grape brûlée 240
Greek salad 87
grilled dishes 7
    fruit kebabs 237
    peaches & cream 235
    scallops & prawns with citrus butter
      191
guacamole 69

H
haddock
    in a cheese jacket 173
    Finnan 177
ham & asparagus rolls 137
honey & nut nests 219
honey-glazed chicken 160
hummus 68

I
Indian dishes
    cod with tomatoes 206
    mango dessert 222
Indonesian sweetcorn balls 118
Italian chocolate truffles 227

K
kebabs
    beef 123
    grilled fruit 237
    grilled scallops & prawns 191
    scallops on skewers 190

L
lamb
    with bay & lemon 141
    with olives 140
    & rice soup 34
    Spanish cutlets 138
    stir-fried 143
leek & chicken soup 38
lemon
    posset 242
    soufflé 251
lentil pâté 90
lobster thermidor 193

M
Madeira sauce 136
mascarpone & spinach soup 23

Mediterranean cod 184
menu-planning 10
Mexican tomato salad 82
monkfish in ruby grapefruit sauce 179
mozzarella & tomatoes 75
mushrooms
    Calabrian soup 18
    & noodle soup 36
    sauce 135
    soup 30
mussels
    Catalan 208
    Thai fragrant 209

N
Neapolitan dishes
    pork steaks 130
    veal cutlets 148
noodles 9
    with chilli & prawns 188
    & mushroom soup 36
    Singapore 107

O
old English cheese soup 26
omelettes
    Chinese 56
    with fines herbes 113
    wild mushroom 112
onions
    gravy 144
    soup 44
orange sauce 126, 155

P
pan-fried scallops & prawns 47
partan bree 39
pasta 9
    fillets of red mullet 198
    fresh spaghetti & meatballs 146
    prawn bake 204
    spaghetti alla carbonara 100
    tagliarini with gorgonzola 51
    & tomato soup 19
pâtés
    lentil 90
    smoked fish & potato 92
pea soup 24
peaches & mascarpone 231
peanut fritters 119
pepper salad 48
pineapple bake 232

pork
    in creamy mushroom sauce 135
    with fennel & juniper 131
    Neapolitan steaks 130
    Singapore noodles 107
    stir-fry 132
    Thai golden pouches 61
    toad in the hole 144
    Virginian chops 129
potatoes 9
    & beef soup 35
    cheese fritters 108
    Russian salad 88
    & smoked fish pâté 92
    veal Italienne 150
prawns
    in anchovy sauce 194
    antipasto volente 66
    balti 203
    flambéed 50
    gamberi fritti 196
    grilled 191
    noodles with chilli 188
    pan-fried 47
    pasta bake 204
    sesame toasts 54
    Singapore noodles 107
    Thai curry 202
prosciutto & figs 74
pumpkin soup 16

R
raspberry fusilli 214
red lentil soup with yogurt 42
red mullet & pasta 198
rice
    Caribbean cook-up 103
    & lamb soup 34
    speedy vegetable pilau 104
ruby grapefruit sauce 179
Russian salad 88

S
salade Niçoise 81
salads 7
    Caesar 85
    chef's 86
    dressings 13
    Greek 87
    Mexican tomato 82
    pepper 48
    Russian 88

salmon with watercress cream 180
sauces
    anchovy 194
    black butter 185
    cheese 137
    creamy mushroom 135
    Hollandaise 114
    Madeira 136
    onion gravy 144
    orange 126, 155
    ready-made 8
    ruby grapefruit 179
    watercress cream 180
scallops
    on horseback 46
    pan-fried 47
    & prawns with citrus butter 191
    on skewers 190
sesame
    ginger chicken 76
    prawn toasts 54
shallots à la Grecque 94
Singapore noodles 107
skate in black butter sauce 185
smoked fish
    & potato pâté 92
    trout with pears 53
sole meunière 183
Somerset pears 223
soups
    artichoke 22
    Calabrian mushroom 18
    carrot & orange 27
    chicken & leek 38
    chunky potato & beef 35
    cream of pea 24
    lamb & rice 34
    mushroom 30
    mushroom & noodle 36
    old English cheese 26
    partan bree 39
    pumpkin 16
    red lentil with yogurt 42
    spicy crab 33
    spicy dahl & carrot 40
    spinach & mascarpone 23
    thick onion 44
    tomato 28
    tomato & pasta 19
    vegetable & bean 20
    yogurt & spinach 43
    zuppa pavese 31

spaghetti
    alla carbonara 100
    & meatballs 146
Spanish cutlets 138
speedy vegetable pilau 104
spicy dishes
    crab soup 33
    dahl & carrot soup 40
    sweetcorn fritters 58
spinach
    & mascarpone soup 23
    & yogurt soup 43
steak in orange sauce 126
stir-fries 7
    chicken teriyaki 157
    lamb 143
    pork 132
stock 13
storecupboard tuna 111
stores 6, 7–8, 10
strawberry baked Alaska 241
stuffed tomatoes 116
sugar-topped fruit cake 212
sweetcorn
    Indonesian balls 118
    spicy fritters 58

T

tagliarini with gorgonzola 51
tarragon chicken 161
Thai dishes
    fragrant mussels 209
    golden pouches 61
    prawn curry 202
thick onion soup 44
Thousand Island Dressing 13
time-saving tips 7–9, 12
tiramisu 215
toad in the hole with onion gravy 144
toffee pudding 245
tomatoes
    fried green 117
    Mexican salad 82
    & mozzarella 75
    & pasta soup 19
    paste 8–9
    soup 28
    stuffed 116
tournedos Rossini 125
trout
    with almonds 176
    with pears 53

with smoked bacon 200
tuna
    antipasto volente 66
    storecupboard 111
turkey breasts with orange sauce 155
Tuscan puddings 218

V
vanilla ice cream 230
veal
    Italienne 150
    Neapolitan cutlets 148
    in a rose petal sauce 152
vegetables 7
    & bean soup 20
    peelers 11
    ready-prepared 8
    speedy pilau 104
    stock 13
vegetarian fajitas 71
veiled country lass 249
Veracruz red snapper 186
vinaigrette 13
Virginian pork chops 129

W
Western dishes 6
wild mushroom omelettes 112

Y
yogurt
    red lentil soup 42
    & spinach soup 43
York ham & asparagus rolls 137

Z
zabaglione 234
zuppa pavese 31